In Another World With My Smartphone

14

Patora Fuyuhara
illustration・Eiji Usatsuka

Luli

The fourth of Touya's summoned Heavenly Beasts. She is the Azure Monarch, the ruler of dragons. She often clashes with Kohaku due to her condescending personality.

Kougyoku

The third of Touya's summoned Heavenly Beasts. She is the Flame Monarch, ruler of feathered things. Though her appearance is flashy and extravagant, she's actually quite cool and collected.

Sango and Kokuyou

The second of Touya's summoned Heavenly Beasts. They are the Black Monarch, two in one. The rulers of scaled beasts. They can freely manipulate water. Sango is a tortoise, and Kokuyou is a snake. Sango is a female, and Kokuyou is a male (but he's very much a female at heart).

Kohaku

The first of Touya's summoned Heavenly Beasts. She's the White Monarch, the ruler of beasts, the guardian of the West and a beautiful White Tiger. She can create devastating shockwaves, and also change size at will.

High Rosetta

Terminal Gynoid in charge of the Workshop, one of the Babylon relics. She's called Rosetta for short. Her Airframe Serial Number is #27. For whatever reason, she's the most reliable of the bunch.

Francesca

Terminal Gynoid in charge of the Hanging Garden, one of the Babylon relics. She's called Cesca for short. Her Airframe Serial Number is #23. She likes to tell very inappropriate jokes.

Mochizuki Moroha

The God of Swords. Claims to be Touya's older sister. She trains and advises the knights of Brunhild. She's gallant and brave, but also a bit of an airhead at times.

Mochizuki Karen

The God of Love. Claims to be Touya's older sister. She stays in Brunhild because she says she needs to catch a servile god, but doesn't really do all that much in the way of hunting him. She's a total pain in the butt.

Pamela Noel

Terminal Gynoid in charge of the Tower, one of the Babylon relics. She's called Noel for short and wears a jersey. Her Airframe Serial Number is #25. She sleeps all the time, and eats lying down. Her tremendous laziness means she doesn't do all that much.

Preliora

Terminal Gynoid in charge of the Rampart, one of the Babylon relics. She's called Liora for short and wears a blazer. Her Airframe Serial Number is #20. She's the oldest of the Babylon Gynoids, and would attend to the... personal night-time needs of Doctor Babylon herself. She has no experience with men.

Fredmonica

Terminal Gynoid in charge of the Hangar, one of the Babylon relics. She's called Monica for short. Her Airframe Serial Number is #28. She's a funny little hard worker who has a bit of a casual streak. She's a good friend of Rosetta, and is the Gynoid with the most knowledge of the Frame Gears.

Bell Flora

Terminal Gynoid in charge of the Alchemy Lab, one of the Babylon relics. She's called Flora for short and wears a nurse outfit. Her Airframe Serial Number is #21. A nurse with dangerously big boobs and even more dangerous medicines.

Doctor Regina Babylon

An ancient genius from a lost civilization, reborn into an artificial body that resembles a small girl. She is the "Babylon" that created the many artifacts and forgotten technologies scattered around the world today. Her Airframe serial number is #29. she remained in stasis for five-thousand years before finally being awakened.

Atlantica

Terminal Gynoid in charge of the Research Lab, one of the Babylon relics. She's called Tica for short. Her Airframe serial number is #22. Of the Babylon Numbers, she is the one who best embodies Doctor Babylon's inappropriately perverse side.

Lileleparshe

Terminal Gynoid in charge of the Storehouse, one of the Babylon relics. She's called Parshe for short and wears a shrine maiden outfit. Her Airframe Serial Number is #26. She's tremendously clumsy, even if she's just trying to help. The amount of stuff she ruins is troublingly high.

Irisfam

Terminal Gynoid in charge of the Library, one of the Babylon relics. She's called Fam for short and wears a school uniform. Her Airframe Serial Number is #24. She's a total book fanatic and hates being interrupted when she's reading.

Character Profiles

Elze Silhoueska

One of Touya's fiancees.
The elder of the twin sisters saved by Touya some time ago. A ferocious melee fighter, she makes use of gauntlets in combat. Her personality is fairly to-the-point and blunt. She can make use of Null fortification magic, specifically the spell [Boost]. She loves spicy foods.

Yumina Urnea Belfast

One of Touya's fiancees.
Princess of the Belfast Kingdom. She was twelve years old in her initial appearance, and her eyes are heterochromatic. The right is blue, while the left is green. She has mystic eyes that can discern the true character of an individual. She has three magical aptitudes: Earth, Wind, and Darkness. She's also extremely proficient with a bow and arrow. She fell in love with Touya at first sight.

Mochizuki Touya

A highschooler who was accidentally murdered by God. He's a no-hassle kind of guy who likes to go with the flow. He's not very good at reading the atmosphere, and typically makes rash decisions that bite him in the ass. His mana pool is limitless, he can flawlessly make use of every magical element, and he can cast any Null spell that he wants. He's currently the Grand Duke of Brunhild.

Sushie Urnea Ortlinde

One of Touya's fiancees.
She was ten years old in her initial appearance. Her nickname is Sue. The niece of Belfast's king, and Yumina's cousin. Touya saved her from being attacked on the road. She has an innocently adventurous spirit.

Lucia Leah Regulus

One of Touya's fiancees.
The Third Princess of the Regulus Empire, she's Yumina's age. She fell in love with Touya when he saved her during a coup. She likes to fight with twin blades, and she's on good terms with Yumina.

Kokonoe Yae

One of Touya's fiancees.
A samurai girl from the far eastern land of Eashen, a country much like Japan. She tends to repeat herself and speak formally, she does. Yae is quite a glutton, eating more than most normal people would dare touch. She's a hard worker, but can sometimes slack off. Her family runs a dojo back in Eashen, and they take great pride in their craft. It's not obvious at first, but her boobs are pretty big.

Linze Silhoueska

One of Touya's fiancees.
The younger of the twin sisters saved by Touya some time ago. She wields magic, specifically from the schools of Light, Water, and Fire. She finds talking to people difficult due to her own shy nature, but she is known to be surprisingly bold at times. Rumors say she might be the kind of girl who enjoys male on male romance... She loves sweet foods.

Paula

A stuffed toy bear animated by years upon years of the [Program] spell. She's the result of two-hundred years of programmed commands, making her seem like a fully aware living being. Paula... Paula's the worst!

Sakura

A mysterious girl Touya rescued in Eashen. She had lost her memories, but has now finally gotten them back. Her true identity is Farnese Forneus, daughter of the Xenoahs Overlord. Currently living a peaceful life in Brunhild, and she has joined the ranks of Touya's fiancees.

Leen

One of Touya's fiancees.
Former Clan Matriarch of the Fairies, she now serves as Brunhild's Court Magician. She claims to be six-hundred-and-twelve years old, but looks tremendously young. She can wield every magical element except Darkness, meaning her magical proficiency is that of a genius. Leen is a bit of a light-hearted bully.

Hildegard Minas Lestia

One of Touya's fiancees.
First Princess of the Knight Kingdom Lestia. Her swordplay talents earned her a reputation as a 'Knight Princess.' Touya saved her life when she was attacked by a group of Phrase, and she's loved him ever since. She's a good friend of Yae, and she stammers a bit when flustered.

IN ANOTHER WORLD WITH MY SMARTPHONE: VOLUME 14
by Patora Fuyuhara

Translated by Andrew Hodgson
Edited by DxS
Layout by Leah Waig
English Cover & Lettering by Carl Vanstiphout

Copyright © 2018 Patora Fuyuhara
Illustrations by Eiji Usatsuka

Original Japanese edition published in 2018 by Hobby Japan
This English edition is published by arrangement with Hobby Japan, Tokyo

English translation © 2018 J-Novel Club LLC

Find more books like this one at www.j-novel.club!

President and Publisher: Samuel Pinansky
Managing Editor (Novels): Aimee Zink
QA Manager: Hannah N. Carter
Marketing Manager. Stephanie Hii

ISBN: 978-1-7183-5013-7
Printed in Korea
First Printing: February 2021
10 9 8 7 6 5 4 3 2 1

Contents

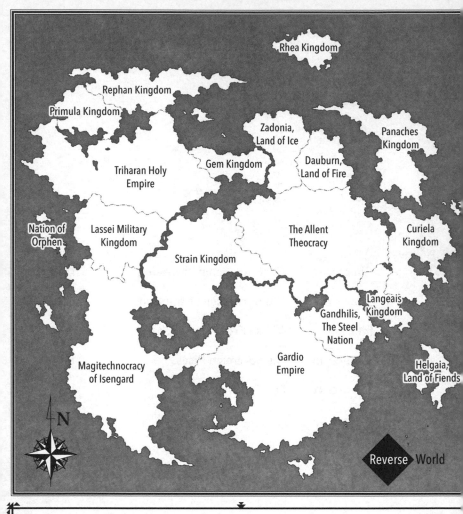

The Story So Far!

Mochizuki Touya, wielding a smartphone customized by God himself, continues to live his life in a new world. After many adventures, Touya, now Grand Duke of a small nation named Brunhild, has joined forces with the other world leaders. Why? To stop the incoming extradimensional threat known as the Phrase, merciless invaders from another world who will stop at nothing until they get what they desire. As Touya continued to investigate potential ways to repel this threat, he found himself falling into another world entirely. This Reverse World was like a mirrored version of the world he knew, and relied on a mysterious mechanical technology known as the Gollems. Now the fate of two worlds may hang in the balance...

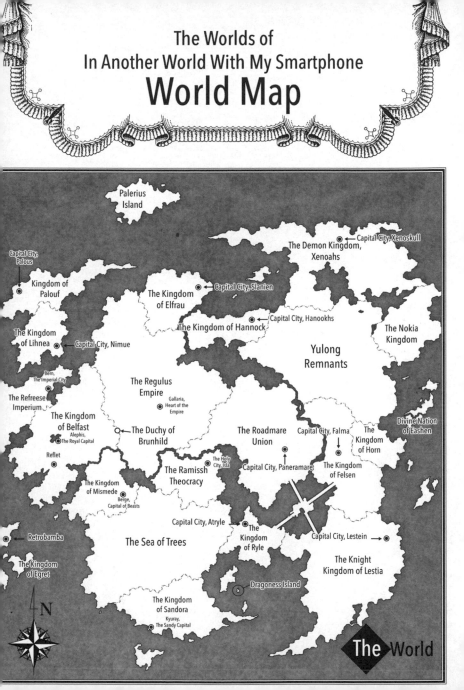

"Pirates, eh? That's no good."

"Quite… Right at the beginning of peak trade season, at that. If we end up missing this opportunity, it'll be quite the financial blow… I'm truly irritated right now, if I must be honest." Olba grumbled quietly to himself as his fox ears twitched and swished.

I'd dropped by the Strand Company building in Brunhild, and Olba happened to be there. We decided to have a small tea break in the back room.

The head office of the Strand Company was located in Berge, Mismede's capital city.

Olba himself didn't conduct operations out of Mismede, though, and most of their trade was primarily conducted via ships.

The Great Gau River connected Belfast, Regulus, Ramissh, Roadmare, Ryle, Felsen, and Lestia… So the ships he sent out would proceed down that route, which he called Route A. Lihnea, Refreese, Palouf, and Elfrau weren't connected along the river, so there was a separate sea-based Route B for trade with those nations.

The sea-based trade route had currently been falling victim to pirates. They'd already lost several ships. That was a major cause for concern.

"We assume their hideout is on one of the islands along Refreese's coast, but they've been pretty good at eluding us so far."

"Can't Refreese do anything about it?"

"Their naval forces have been keeping a keen eye, but… Well, it's not like they can escort our ships all the way."

I took out my smartphone and pulled up the map of the sea from Refreese to Lihnea.

"Search. Pirate hideout."

"Searching… Search complete. Displaying." A few pings ran out as the pin markers landed on several small islands. There were six results in total. I wondered if that meant there were six hideouts that belonged to one band or six separate pirate crews.

"Oh my…"

"Yep, here's the hideouts. I don't think they'd have bothered installing any barriers, so this is probably the lot." I used my camera to screenshot the map, then made a call to the emperor of Refreese.

"Ah, 'sup. Is this the emperor? Yeah, calling about the pirates. Yep… Yep… Gotcha. Oh, sure. I've discovered their hideouts, so I'll send you a photo of the map, alright? No, really… Don't worry about it. Oh, really? Well, maybe later then… Alright, thanks. Glad I could help!"

And that was that.

"Refreese's navy is headed to the hideouts right away. That should help, right?"

"Ah, I… Good grief… You just snapped your fingers and solved such a plague on my company… You're really something else, young man…" Olba let out a heavy sigh as he sipped his drink. I was getting used to this kind of thing, so I just ignored it and sipped my own.

"By the way, Olba, I have a proposition for you."

"Hmm? Your ideas are always welcome, Grand Duke… What's on your mind?" I picked up my smartphone and played a video of the Dverg that Rosetta and the others had repaired the other day.

Rosetta was piloting it as it slowly walked toward a large boulder and picked it up.

"Hm...? Is this a Frame Gear? No, it's smaller..."

"This is a magic construction vehicle created by the Dwarves. It's called a Dverg. It's inferior to the Frame Gears, but more than capable of manual labor. It's still in the testing phase but I wanted to know if you'd be willing to invest."

"Invest...? You wish for me to provide development funds?"

"That's right. In exchange, the Strand Company will have exclusive rights to the machine and its sales. Not a bad deal, is it?" The Dwarves seemed fine with those terms. They said they didn't care too much about profiting, they just wanted to show the world the marvels of Dwarven engineering.

They probably didn't even give any thought to the problems that a national monopoly of that kind of tech could cause.

They only had one condition, which was that Olba would sell the machines to any country, all at the same price.

The raw material cost to construct one was definitely high, so it's not as if any one nation would be able to amass too many. Not to mention the fact that I was the only one with access to the workshop, so mass-producing them would be impossible anywhere else.

If the Dverg ended up becoming a globally-known product, it was possible that other Dwarves around the world could try to produce more on their own, so we needed a proper stake in the market.

"Hmm... I could certainly see this being profitable if my people had a monopoly on it..." Olba leaned forward and muttered to himself as he watched the video play.

"...Very well, then. I'm certainly interested, I just have concerns about the investment cost..."

"If you want to talk it over with the inventors, you can. They're staying at the Silver Moon right now. They know about you, so you'd just have to introduce yourself." Olba seemed a little surprised they were so close, but he quickly straightened himself up and smiled.

"My, my... You've already arranged so much. Did you not consider that I might have said no?"

"Not in the least. A shrewd guy like you, Olba? You'd always be on the ball with this kind of potential profit."

"Hoho, I see. Well, you were quite right." Olba grinned a little as his eyes narrowed on me. All I wanted to do was mediate between him and the dwarves, now all they had to do was iron out the rest. There was nothing in it for me, but I had a feeling that the Dverg would end up becoming a useful excavation and construction tool for those who couldn't use Earth magic. In that regard, it would end up bettering the world.

Olba said he'd visit the Dwarves the following morning, so I said goodbye and left the building.

I opened up a [Gate] and headed up to the Babylon Garden. Doc Babylon and Rosetta were there tuning up the Dimensional Disruptor.

There were new parts installed around the gate's arch.

"Did you finish the adjustments?"

"Basically, yeah. We can trigger it with a lot less magic than before, and we've removed the weight limitations. If I had a little more free time, I'd make further adjustments, but this'll do for now," Doctor Babylon said as she shrugged her shoulders and stashed her gear into the toolbox.

I touched the disruptor to test out her claims, and the meter filled up with far less effort than before. The new parts began to whir and spin.

"Did you finish making the mana tank for the other side, too?"

"That I did, yes. But that's no big deal. Both Dimensional Disruptors are connected by Space-time magic, so improvements to one will be applied to the other." *Wonder if we should go to the other side, then... I did promise everyone they could come.*

I needed to cast [**Translation**] on everyone first, though.

That spell was useful because I could use it to teach others languages that I'd absorbed.

I wasn't able to communicate with dragons using it, though. Apparently, they communicated with some kind of unique telepathy.

To be honest, though, I didn't really want to learn the languages of monsters and animals. I definitely didn't want to hear the opinions of chickens, cows, and other livestock.

Either way, there was no point fretting. I had a trip to arrange.

I went to the research laboratory to pick up the new mana tank and reactivate the three etoiles. I'd noticed that the three of them were wearing petite maid uniforms; Tica had likely been responsible for it... But it did suit them, so it was okay.

Once I got back to the Garden with the three etoiles, everyone was already gathered and ready.

Even Sue had come, all the way from Belfast. With the professor included, I wondered if all ten of us plus Paula and the etoiles would be alright over there.

I sent word to Kousaka and told him not to worry about our absence. Ideally, I'd want to be back in Brunhild by the evening, but there was no way of guaranteeing that due to the time dilation.

According to Doctor Babylon, her tune-up on the Dimensional Disruptor reduced the amount of time it took to traverse worlds, but we wouldn't know by how much until we went and gave it a go.

I channeled my magic through the tank, and the Dimensional Disruptor opened up a portal.

"Well then... Let's go... Could you maybe let go of my coat, though?" Everyone there was holding on to me tightly, except for Doctor Babylon. I could understand their unease.

"T-Touya-dono... I am simply afraid that we might be separated, I am..."

"H-Holding on to you is fine, right?" Elze and Linze were clinging to my right arm, while Lu tightly clasped my right hand. Hilde and Yae were on the opposite side, seizing my left arm as Yumina grabbed my left hand. Leen and Sakura were clinging to my waist on either side, and Sue had clambered up to my back... Paula was sitting on my head. I felt like a heavily-armored knight.

Still, I only had to bear with it while we passed through, so it would be fine.

We passed through the Dimensional Disruptor, slowly but surely. The sensation of walking through a rubbery material was there again, but it was easier to move through. It was probably because of Babylon's improvements. We made it through and came out into the garden on Drakliff Island. I looked around and found myself rather surprised at what I saw.

There was a beautiful stone pathway leading from the portal and beautiful flowers in bloom all around us. The garden had been decorated since I last left, and it was clearly well-attended and gorgeous.

"Wow, this is so pretty!" Sue jumped down from my back and ran to the flowerbed. Yumina and Lu followed suit as Paula clambered from the top of my head.

Hm... Everyone seems fine, then... Guess the Dimensional Disruptor works well.

"Yae, there are so many dragons…"

"You are correct, Hilde-dono…" Yae and Hilde stood at the edge of the cliff and watched a group of wyverns fly by.

Well, this is a dragon island, so what do you expect? But… Who did that with my garden? Oh wait, could this be that silver dragon's work…?

"Greetings, everyone. It's a pleasure to meet you." As if appearing to answer my question, Shirogane suddenly came to greet us.

He was wearing a formal black butler suit with white gloves, and his long silver hair was tied with string. *What the hell, man! You look really hot!* Shirogane bowed his head to me. His posture was definitely on point. I grumbled quietly about how jealous I was of his good looks before introducing him to everyone.

"Everyone, this is Shirogane. He's in charge of this house while I'm away. He might look like a beastman, but he's actually a Silver Dragon that can take human form."

"My name is Shirogane, indeed. It's a pleasure." Everyone stared at him with a look of confusion on their faces. Then I realized what I'd done. I'd forgotten to cast the linguistic magic on them, so they couldn't understand a word he was saying.

"**[Translation].**" I cast the spell and everyone was suddenly able to understand him without any issues.

I then introduced all the girls as my fiancees, except for Doctor Babylon. She kept insisting that she was my mistress, but I refused to let that slide.

"So, what's up with the garden?"

"Ah, yes! I was told I could do as I wished, so I did some decorating."

So it was you, you sure are a dragon of many talents… I'm pretty surprised you have such a green thumb… But I guess Silver Dragons are just weirdos.

"Now then, please come inside. Right this way sir, and madams."

They're not married to me yet... But they certainly seem happy with his manner of address... Guess we've got ourselves quite the butler.

The interior was gaudier than it was when I'd left it. There was a Leylight stone chandelier, a magnificent carpet, a cupboard, potted plants, paintings, fully functional blackout curtains, and even several comfy beds. Everything had been arranged perfectly.

"You sure had fun, huh..."

"I'd never had the chance to shop in a human town before, so... Well, I went a little wild, but I thought your home would be best fitted with fine furnishings." He certainly wasn't wrong about the fine part, since everything looked amazing. I had nothing to complain about, at least.

"Touya, there's even a library!" Linze had discovered a book-filled room, which certainly got her excited. Leen picked up a book and began flipping through it with curious eyes... Doctor Babylon followed suit.

"You bought books, too?"

"Of course. I haven't had contact with humanity in over two-hundred years, so I purchased enough to really get myself up to speed." That made sense. There were a lot of different genres, too. He'd picked up history books, technical manuals, war stories, and even academic textbooks. I even saw a couple of cookbooks... Which made me wonder if dragons even needed to cook. I left the library and headed to the living room. There was a big comfy couch and a table with a beautiful flower vase on top. There was a nice-looking clock on the wall, too. Not to mention the very fancy and expensive-looking chest of drawers up against the wall.

I sat down on the couch and practically sank into it, it was really nice.

"Please, do relax. I'll bring tea." Shirogane bowed and left the room.

"He's a pretty good butler, huh? But I dunno if he's as good as mine!" Sue grinned slightly as she sat herself down next to me. He wasn't as talented at butlering as Leim, that much was sure... Laim would give him a run for his money, too.

"So, what are we going to do? We wanted to leave by the evening, right?"

"That's right. I was wondering if you might take us to a capital city." Lu sat down next to me as she answered my question.

Capitals, huh...? Well, there's Allen... Or there's Goldose... I guess I haven't actually been anywhere except those places.

If we wanted to have a fun day out, then Goldose was the place to go, but I felt uneasy about that place since the attack on the black market. That's why I decided that Allen was the best place for us to go.

I didn't want to run into Nia or the Red Cats... So I hoped that they'd stay in their forest hideout for at least today.

I didn't want my fiancees finding out that I'd peeked at her panties, after all.

"Is there something on your mind, Touya-dono, is there?"

"Ah, no... Nothing." I smiled over at Yae, who was eyeing me suspiciously.

Alright, we'll head off to Allen. The only people I know there are Mr. Sancho and the Red Cats, so I guess just strolling around the place should be decent fun.

We drank the tea that Shirogane brought in (it was great) as I explained my idea. Everyone except Doctor Babylon said they'd tag along. She wanted to make some final tweaks to the Dimensional Disruptor Mk. II and install the mana tank.

I also asked Shirogane to take care of the three Gollems. I didn't really expect him to teach them anything weird, so I figured it would be fine.

They only followed orders given to them by their master, so I just ordered them to listen to Shirogane as well.

"We'll be heading out, then. We expect to be back by evening."

"Very well. Have a pleasant and safe trip!"

"Ping."

"Pong."

"Pang." The three etoiles mimicked Shirogane's bowing motion. That's when I was certain that leaving them with him was probably a good idea.

I opened up a [Gate] to the capital city, Allen.

We came out into the main street and saw people and their Gollems walking by.

There was a man riding a Gollem that resembled a small Dverg, as it hauled a cart behind it. Just as I watched them pass by, a massive, armored, two-and-a-half meter Gollem walked past us alongside a young knight.

"Oh my... It really is another world..."

"...Wow..." Hilde and Sakura murmured quietly as they watched all the different Gollems walk by.

The others timidly followed after me as I walked. We must've looked pretty backwater.

Paula's tottering caught the attention of a few people, but they lost interest relatively quickly. People probably just thought she was another Gollem. Frankly, I was glad we weren't standing out too much.

"I guess we should go visit Mr. Sancho... I could do with some money, after all."

"Is he the merchant that helped you, Touya?"

"That's right. I'll have him buy some gold and silver from me." The money I'd made from the Red Cats had mostly been used to buy the three Gollems, after all. We still had enough to eat well, but I wanted some more money so everyone could buy themselves a nice souvenir. More money was always better than less, in the end.

We arrived at Mr. Sancho's store when I saw the man himself talking to a few merchants. Their faces looked a little dire.

"Ahh, it's you, Tohya! Did you need something?"

"Good day to you, Mr. Sancho. I was looking to see if you'd buy, but… Is something wrong?"

"Ah, well… We were just discussing the incident, you know? They say someone got away from Geore Village just in time…"

"Hm? What incident?" I was confused, but Mr. Sancho just looked at me like he was surprised.

"You don't know? But everyone's been talking about it! It's even in the newspapers…"

"Ah, sorry… I haven't been here for a while."

There are newspapers in this world? Oh, the Red Cats did have a comms device, so maybe this world has decent information technology… The regular world only has communication artifacts and horses…

Oh, I guess the other world does have bulletin boards for general news, though.

"Ah, I see… If you weren't around the city, then it makes sense you wouldn't know! Look here."

Mr. Sancho showed me the paper. I looked at it with some surprise. It was stiff, and the paper quality wasn't exactly very good. The printing looked neat, but the paper itself was about half the size of the newspapers back on Earth.

I looked down at the main headline and instinctively caught my own breath.

'Golden Monster Sighted In Geore!' There was an illustration beneath, a realistic likeness of the creature that had been spotted. At a glance, it kind of resembled a ladybug, but it was clearly well-rounded and had various limbs. There was no mistaking it, I'd seen this creature before.

"...One of the mutant Phrase..." It was a golden monster alright. There was no mistaking it, this was a drawing of one of the metal devils. One of the wicked god's dependents.

◇　◇　◇

The newspaper had the following to say about the incident:

A golden monster appeared all of a sudden in Geore Village, not far from the Holy Capital. The monster attacked the villagers and began ripping them apart, one by one.

A few survivors escaped, but only barely. The Knight Order responded to the summons and charged in with their Gollem Enforcers.

What they found when they arrived at the village was the golden monster and several crystal skeletons shambling around the streets. The knights engaged the creature and met success against the skeletons, but even the Skills of the Gollems were ineffective against the golden creature, and so they had to go on the defensive.

The prince of the Panaches Kingdom just happened to be passing by, and he used the power of his crown Gollem to destroy the golden creature.

Then the monster completely dissolved into a liquid, leaving behind the mystery of just what it was. The Allent Theocracy was now developing countermeasures in case another decided to appear.

"…Well, isn't that just fine and dandy." I had Mr. Sancho buy a few more ingots from me, said my goodbyes, and took the girls with me to a nearby cafe.

"I understand how you must feel, but it's bad manners to read while eating. Could you not, for now?"

"Hm? Ah… Sorry…" Leen scolded me lightly because I was holding a sandwich in one hand and a newspaper in the other. Apparently, I'd been reading longer than I thought because everyone else was done eating.

Yumina, having finished her food, took the newspaper from me.

"Hm… It really is one of them, isn't it?"

"I'm pretty sure, yeah… And judging from what the paper says, it must've eaten its victims' souls."

"But why wasn't it a regular Phrase? Why did one of the mutants come to this world?" Lu tilted her head to the side. I had a general idea, though.

"The Phrase exist to seek out their Sovereign, right? That's why they came to our home. Because the Sovereign lives inside a living person in that world. That's also why they've been killing people in our world. But the metal devils don't play by those rules." I remembered how they even attacked a Dominant Construct like Gila. Those creatures couldn't even be called Phrase anymore.

"Basically, it would be stupid to expect regular Phrase in this world. There's no reason for them to come here, after all. But those mutated versions… Maybe they have an objective here." That was the best kind of conclusion to make for the time being. They were probably obeying orders from the wicked god, the creature that had consumed that NEET god.

That made sense, but there was still part of this whole thing that concerned me.

The regular world, the one I'd come from, was freely invaded by the Phrase due to the damaged world barrier... But the Reverse World should have had a fully functioning barrier. The appearance of a metal devil meant that it was potentially no longer intact.

Either way, they were here. At least one of them. They'd appeared in our world first, and now this one... I wondered if something had happened in the gap between worlds, but I had no way of telling.

I was worried that Yula and the wicked god might have been planning something dangerous, but it wasn't like I could do anything about it.

Still... What are they playing at with covert actions across two worlds...?

"...Touya?"

"Hm? Ah... What?" *Crap, I ended up getting lost in thought again.* I apologized to Yumina for worrying her, and quietly resigned myself to fate for the time being.

I wolfed down the remains of my sandwich and washed it back with my now-cold tea.

I was curious about this crown that had killed the metal devil. It wasn't Nia's Red Crown or Luna's Purple Crown... The paper had mentioned some prince.

I wondered what price the prince needed to pay in order to use his crown... Defeating a Phrase definitely required some incredible power, after all...

He must have had to pay some kind of appropriate compensation. But I remembered what Nia had said, that aside from the Purple Crown, all crowns could be used without risk of death...

But if the cost was something like making your feet permanently smell worse with each use, that would still be really bad.

I looked on my map and found that the Panaches Kingdom was located around the area where Palouf and Lihnea were located in the regular world, on Palnea Island. The whole island seemed to be unified as one nation in the Reverse World.

I then used my map to run a search for any Phrase or metal devils, but nothing came up.

I felt crappy, but there was nothing to be done... I decided to change the mood a bit. "We came this far, so how about we do some shopping? We might even find something rare or unusual! We have money, so let's give it a shot! I'll hold the bags, too!"

I didn't want the girls feeling uneasy, so I shifted gears. Even though I said I'd hold the bags, I was actually just gonna toss them into [Storage].

"Oh, that's right! I wanna buy souvenirs for my father and mother and the old man as well!" Sue grinned broadly, but I reminded her not to tell anyone where she got the gifts from.

"Sounds good to me. Shall we go?"

"I would like to find a new drinking cup, I would."

"And I'd like to visit a bookstore."

"I'd like to see what armors I could find in this world." Everyone brought up what they were after, so I used my smartphone to find various stores of interest. Then we all set off.

But I underestimated them... Or rather, I underestimated the terrifying power of the female shopper.

The carrying part was fine, thanks to my [Storage] spell, but I was waiting around forever. They also kept asking my opinion... I didn't want to be too blunt, so it was a lot of agonizing and me just telling them what they wanted to hear... It was a hellish experience, multiplied by nine...

Plus this happened with every store we went into. They didn't ask my opinion about everything, but it kept happening nonetheless. It was even worse in clothing stores.

We went to shoe stores, hat stores, accessory stores, weapon stores, bookstores, grocery stores, furniture stores, general stores, musical stores, jewelry stores, makeup stores, bakeries… I ended up losing count of how many stores we hit.

I finally found myself at a store that specialized in ladies' undergarments. Naturally, I wasn't going to go in with them, and they weren't going to ask for my thoughts… So I was stuck waiting outside.

I didn't want people mistaking me for some kind of pervert, so I moved away from the storefront and stood on a street corner near a blacksmith's.

The blacksmith was hard at work repairing some armored plating on a Gollem, which led me to assume that kind of thing was standard in this world.

The Gollem's upper body was that of a minotaur, but its lower body had tracks like a tank. I'd have probably called it a Minotank. It was tough and rugged, which meant it was probably built for power. It also had a weapon on its person, a massive double-edged ax.

The blacksmith gave me permission to watch him work, so I decided to spend time watching him do his job.

"Do you get many Gollem repair jobs?"

"Well, sonny. We ain't exactly Gollem Engineers… I'd say the most we can do is fix the outer plating. The factory models are also pretty simple to tweak if their arms or legs get messed up. Oh, we make weapons an' armor for them, too." *That's pretty cool… I guess I didn't think about how Gollems would interact with blacksmiths.*

I looked around and saw an object in the corner of the room.

It looked like a vaguely familiar piece of equipment. It was about forty centimeters in diameter... It sure looked like a mana furnace to me.

"What's that...?"

"Hm? Oh, the Magic Motor? It's part of a Gollem Carriage that I recently dismantled. We didn't need it, so I was thinking of selling it fer cheap. It's old."

I used [**Analyze**] to confirm the information. It was pretty much identical to the one we used in the Dverg. Except it was a lot more compact and had a relatively smaller magical output due to the fact that it didn't incorporate spellstones. I wondered if that meant we could make our own Gollem-like creations; we could probably use Spellstones and Ether Liquid to make up for the lack of a G-Cube.

I tested the device, taking care not to break it like I did last time, and it whirred slightly.

"Hey, can I buy this from you?"

"Hm? Sure... If you like." He was planning on selling it for cheap, so I got it at a decent price... Supposedly. It wasn't like I knew the going prices or anything.

It was possible that I could use this thing to make something like a motorized car.

We had an armored car in the Babylon Hangar, but I didn't really want to mass-produce something with such insane levels of speed and power. It could only be made in our workshop, too.

If I managed to get the magic motor mass produced, then other nations would be able to make them. It would probably only be powerful enough to make a one or two-seater vehicle, though.

I left the blacksmith's and looked across the street to see the girls walking toward me.

"Please forgive us, Touya-dono. We left you waiting, we did."

"No, don't worry... I managed to pick up something good, too."
I smiled toward Yae as I put the magic motor into [Storage]. I offered
to put their bags in as well, but the girls said no. It was probably
because it was underwear... They didn't want me peeking. "Man,
there was a hell of a line in there... Plus, Linze spent ages deciding
whether to go for something more proper, or something more
daring... But in the end, she just went for bo-"

"S-Sis!! Please don't blabber so needlessly!" Linze turned bright
red as she clamped a hand over Elze's mouth.

"Elze-dono was also troubled in deciding, she was. In the end, it
was a one-cup fits a—"

"Auuuuugh!" Elze suddenly slammed her palm over Yae's
mouth. Those girls sure could be silly sometimes.

I decided to keep quiet since I felt like I'd lose no matter what
I said in this situation. *I just need to become like a stone... Focus,
Touya... Turn your mind to steel...*

"...Grand Duke, do you want to see...?" Sakura's words pierced
me through to the core as I tried to remain stoic. I was placed into
checkmate. If I said no, they'd be upset. If I said yes, they'd be upset.
I had no options!

"Something wrong, Touya? Don't you wanna see our underwear?
I don't mind. What about you, Lu?"

"Wh-What?! D-D-Don't drag me into this, Sue... Ah... N-Not
that I wouldn't show you, Touya... B-But... Uhm... W-Wouldn't
you rather see Hilde's?!"

"Huh?! Me?! Wh-Why me?! I bought striped ones, but... Ah...
Wait! I didn't s-say that!" Sue lit the fuse on a bomb and then passed
it along to Lu and Hilde respectively.

Her words were completely innocent, of course. But she
definitely had no filter when it came to stuff she was unaware of. Her

mother, Ellen, was blind for a long time… It made me wonder if her condition meant she hadn't taught Sue about basic social cues.

"Okay, okay. Enough already. This isn't the kind of thing to discuss in the middle of the street. We'll leave it here." Leen clapped her hands together and ordered everyone to stop. I was glad that the eldest of them was taking charge, even if she looked around the same age as Yumina or Lu.

The girls noticed that they were drawing attention and started walking down the street. I sighed and expressed my thanks to Leen.

"They're all a little shy, you know. You need to be a little more commanding, darling. After all, you'll be able to see us in our underwear whenever you want soon enough."

"Gimme a break…" I groaned quietly as Leen took my arm and began to walk alongside me.

"By the way, I chose a frilly black lace set… Would you like to see?"

"…C'mon…" *How would that kind of adult lingerie even look on someone with such a child-like body? Though I guess it doesn't matter what Leen wears, she's still Leen. I'm sure she'll look amazing in any type of clothing she chooses.*

"Well? Want to?"

"I'd be lying if I said no. It's not like I'm not interested… I'm just hesitant to say so outright. If you want to force me to see, then I won't stop you… I just don't have the guts to outright say I want to see yet, that's all."

"Goodness grief, darling… You're quite the handful." I was lying. My intentions weren't even nearly that pure. I just didn't think I'd be able to control myself if I saw someone I loved in clothes like that! *Don't tempt me, you wicked witch! You're always such a tease, Leen! Auuugh!*

"Fufu… You're always so fun to play with, Touya." Leen grinned as she clung tighter to my arm. Sakura turned around and noticed this, before quickly running back and clinging to my other arm.

"No fair… Don't hog all of him…"

Oh geez… This feels nice, but I'm still shy… Knock it off, Paula! Don't make that kind of 'ooh la la' gesture!

She was really full of life, despite her status as a stuffed toy… I was honestly curious about the sheer extent of the programming that had been put into her.

We walked into a back alley and I opened a portal back to Drakliff Island.

"Welcome back."

"Oh, you're finally done."

Shirogane bowed his head to us, and the professor lazily waved while lying back on the couch as she looked up from her book.

"I call it the Ether Vehicle. It's basically a magical automobile."

"Oho…"

"It looks like a carriage…" I was in a small plaza to the north of Brunhild Castle, showing my new invention to the other world leaders. I didn't exactly invent it, but that was just a fine detail.

It had four thin wheels and an open roof, two leather seats and two headlights on the front.

It was outfitted with a steering wheel and a basic horn, as well as accelerators and brake pedals. There was also a sunroof installed that could be manually pulled back.

Specifically, I'd based the Ether Vehicle on a car model from Earth. The Fiat 4 HP. It was a four-wheeled gasoline-powered car produced by the Italian car company, Fiat, way back in 1899.

I brought the magic motor back from the Reverse World, then tasked Rosetta, a group of craftsmen, and the town's blacksmiths with building the car from scratch.

That meant that the body of the car didn't use technology from Babylon, nor the ancient civilization. Which in turn meant that any country with enough money and skill could produce one. They would have to buy the Ether Liquid fuel from Brunhild, though... But that would be fine. The Frame Gears didn't run on it anymore, after all.

The back of the car had a 500ml plastic bottle of Ether Liquid installed. It just looked like melon soda, chilling in the back.

I hopped into the front and fired up the car. The steering wheel started draining some of the magic reserves. It was pretty responsive due to my magical affinity.

After that I hit the accelerator, causing the vehicle to start slowly moving around.

"Ooh!"

"It's moving!" The motor was operated by magic power that was amplified not only by Ether Liquid, but also spellstones installed into the car. That meant that it ran quietly and didn't exhaust the driver. That being said, if someone drove for a full day it would probably wear them out.

Plus, it was good for the environment because there were no gas emissions. There was an exhaust that shot out a steady stream of glittering steam, but that was just waste residue from magic and Ether Liquid and was completely safe.

It could go a little faster than a horse-drawn carriage, but if the horses were galloping then it would probably lose. I had a feeling that future model developments would improve speed and efficiency, though.

I turned the wheel and made an effective U-Turn, and once I was back in front of the other world leaders, I hit the brakes.

"Hmm... It seems to go about the same speed as a carriage, with less of the stress. You won't need to feed or maintain horses, after all..."

"You'll still need to maintain the vehicle itself. Anyone can drive it with enough practice, though. Just uh... Try not to let children drive it, that would be dangerous." I planned on incorporating a lock system that analyzed fingerprints. I didn't want to hear about some five-year-old kid going for a joyride, after all.

"It's certainly less flashy than a Frame Gear, but a lot more convenient as transportation." The King of Lihnea nodded slowly. I felt comparing it to the Frame Gear was unfair, but I figured after they'd been introduced to giant robots, something like a car would seem a little plain.

"Touya, my boy. May I take it for a spin?"

"Go ahead. I'm hoping to introduce these worldwide, so it'd be good if you all got a feel for it." I nodded to the beastking and pulled out four more Ether Vehicles from [Storage].

The king of Belfast and the emperor of Regulus got into the one I'd been riding, the beastking and the overlord got into another, the king of Lihnea and the knight king of Lestia got into the third, the pope of Ramissh and the doge of Roadmare got into the fourth, and the king of Felsen and the young king of Palouf got into the last one.

It was kind of funny seeing the tiny king of Palouf next to such an oversized man.

The cars began to start up. We'd installed safety teleportation features much like the Frame Gears, so I wasn't worried about crashing.

They all slowly began to drive their cars as I looked on with the emperor of Refreese.

"That reminds me, Touya... You really helped out with that pirate matter the other day. The merchants in my region are all thankful."

"Did you take them all out?"

"We did. However... Of the ships that headed out to take care of the pirates, one went missing... We're searching for it, but would it be within your power to locate it?"

"I should be able to do that... Can you describe the ship at all?" I heard a brief description from the emperor and ran a search of the Refreese coastline on my map. There were no hits. That meant it had likely sunk... If it had fallen apart to debris and sank to the bottom of the ocean, then my spell wouldn't be able to pick it up.

"Hmph... I suppose it must have been destroyed by a beast of the sea... Forgive me, Grand Duke, for wasting your time... I shall call off the search." Sea monsters that were capable of sinking ships were usually limited to Krakens and Sea Serpents.

Adventurers were generally fine with taking out monsters on the land, but the world didn't have much it could do against sea-dwelling nasties.

The ship was called The McClane, which made me slightly amused. But it wasn't like the bald-headed emperor next to me would know anything about famous Hollywood movies... It was just a coincidence.

But still, for the ship to bear the name of the world's unluckiest detective... It was a bad omen from the start. If only it had as much will to survive as John McClane had in his movies.

The world leaders were all so pleased with the Ether Vehicles that they asked to buy several each. I was satisfied with how things had gone.

The Ether Liquid that came with the cars would last over half a year, but I gave them all an extra bottle as a bonus. I also threw in some spare tires and off-road wheels. Mismede and Xenoahs had rougher areas, after all.

I also informed them that the cars could be reverse-engineered. If they dismantled them they'd be able to make their own changes. I didn't plan on directly profiting, so I just wanted to see what each country could make of the vehicles in the coming years.

The money earned from the Ether Liquid would be enough, anyway. To be honest, it was possible for the other nations to produce it themselves after enough research, so I was waiting to see if they'd manage it.

"I think we might need to pave the roads a bit more if these vehicles become more commonplace, though..."

"Actually, the Dwarves have recently created a magical construction vehicle that might make that easier. It should allow you to terraform without the use of Earth magic." The development was proceeding as scheduled, and would soon be available on the market. That was all up to Olba, though. He was the one deciding the points of sale and the price. I wasn't really profiting from that, either.

The others continued to ride their cars for a while. It was obvious they were having fun, even if they were trying to pretend it was all formal testing. They even started a little race.

For what it was worth, the young king of Palouf was faster than all the others. It wasn't a matter of skill, though. He was just the lightest.

The next day I made sure to deliver the Ether Vehicles to each nation. They were only allowed to order a maximum of five each. I collected the payment and then took it to Kousaka.

I was looking down at the castle courtyard from my balcony. Lapis and the maids were practicing how to drive the cars.

We'd built a simple race course in the courtyard. It was simple, kind of like the tutorial level in a racing game.

The head maid sure got excited as she hopped into the car, but it didn't really need as much finesse as a bicycle so I was sure she'd be fine.

The controls were simplistic, really. Much like a go-kart. Even a kid could do it, honestly. I probably should've made the controls a little more complex, but it wasn't like we had driving schools or anything.

Lapis started up the car and started to drive slowly. She made a single lap around the course and gradually got used to it. She was driving safely, for the most part. She'd probably be able to take the car out to town, it'd help with shopping runs... Then again, the head maid wasn't really tasked with going out and shopping.

I continued to watch them practice in the courtyard when my smartphone began to ring. The display said it was the overlord of Xenoahs. I wondered if there was an issue with the cars I'd delivered.

"Hey, 'sup?"

"Ah, Grand Duke?"

"Something up? If you're calling to ask about Sakura, I don't really have time."

"Hold on a moment! She's my daughter, and I... Wait, this isn't the time for that..."

"So, what's wrong?"

"That information you gave us some time ago! The mutant variation of the Phrase... Those metal devils? One appeared in my country!"

"What...?!"

A mutant in Xenoahs?!

"It was in a town called Radom. The town was known for being a hive of scum and villainy, crime there happened often... It's the kind of place where negative emotions gather, so it fits the bill for their target."

"What happened to the citizens?"

"All dead. Turned into crystallized zombies. There was only one of the monsters, thankfully. I dispatched the Ogre Squad and they managed to kill it, but not without suffering losses."

Ogre Squad, huh...? I guess one Ogre has the strength of ten men, so it makes sense they'd be able to take it out. Still, it couldn't have been easy...

The fact that crystal skeletons appeared meant that souls had been consumed. The wicked god appeared in Sandora and Lestia to strengthen itself by eating souls... So I was worried that it was another case of that happening. First the Reverse World incident, now this... Clearly, the wicked god was up to something.

It could probably happen again, too. The sensors that the guilds were equipped with could only pick up regular Phrase signals. If we captured a metal devil alive and researched it, we could probably make a separate scanner.

"The dead mutant melted into goop, as we were informed... The skeletons all collapsed once their cores were shattered, too. We collected the pieces, just in case. Are they made of that, er... Phrasium material?"

"On a base level, yeah. They'll harden if you pour magic into the fragments, and they're purer than spellstones. You can't put the fragments together, though, so they'll be largely useless in such small chunks."

"They're valuable, at the very least... But we are hesitant to make use of them, given that they're the remains of the victims... They won't be able to rest in peace, either."

The overlord knew that those who had their souls devoured couldn't reach salvation. They weren't allowed to pass on to the other side, being effectively obliterated and removed from the cycle of reincarnation. It was a pretty horrific fate.

Maybe the wicked god is collecting the soul energy and using it to create the metal devils... I'm honestly getting a little scared of the power it's gradually building...

Either way, Xenoahs had taken care of it, so they were free to do what they wanted with the Phrasium. They would probably trade it for money and pay it out to the families or relatives of the deceased. Alternatively, they could improve their own weapons or armor. Even small fragments could be made into something similar to scale mail.

I ended the call with the overlord. The conversation made me wonder if I needed to start gathering allies in the Reverse World in case any incidents like this happened again.

I sighed and shook my head...

Looking down at the courtyard, I noticed Lapis driving a car at insane speeds toward a corner.

Whoa, holy shit! You're going too fast! You're gonna... What the?! Lapis was somehow making the car glide on its side, causing the vehicle to lean as it cleanly changed its direction without compromising any speed.

She's drifting... Or, wait... She's hanging off? Holy crap! That's crazy...!

I stood, dumbfounded, by how insane her technique was. Frankly, I was getting worried about the tires... She was definitely damaging them.

I started wondering if we could do some kind of street-based grand prix like the Circuit de Monaco.

Either way, the maids of Brunhild were clearly a force to be reckoned with.

"They're in the Pallin Desert within the former Sandora Kingdom's territory… At the very least there are ten-thousand. It's an invasion force similar to the number that appeared in Yulong."

"And when can we expect them?"

"I'd say we have less than a day." I was on the phone with Guildmaster Relisha, quietly concerned about what she was telling me. A large Phrase invasion was incoming.

The only saving grace of the situation was that they were in the desert. Their emergence spot was also several hundred kilometers from Draggah, the nearest town.

Since I liberated the slaves, the region was largely disrupted. Regular farmers and traders who didn't own slaves weren't really affected all that much. I also heard that several of the freed slaves who remained in Sandora had gotten proper employment, as well.

The problem came from the nobles and large-scale merchants that had subjected the slaves to abuse.

They feared that the freed slaves would want to take revenge, so they ended up fleeing the region and taking all their assets with them. Even their guardsmen were slaves, so it wasn't like there were many people available to help them, either.

As a result of the mass exodus of the elite, those that governed the major cities and towns were all gone. The people remaining ended up dividing the territory into city state-like nations.

Among those city-states were even settlements that were founded and built upon by liberated slaves. It wasn't as if every noble was abusive. There were some who remained because they had good relationships with their workers to begin with, even if they were indentured.

Sandora was a dictatorship that didn't interact much with the outside world, so they had good self-sufficiency when it came to things like food. That hadn't changed after the country dissolved, so people were still able to eat. Either way, the nobles had gone and the lower classes were running the place in their own way.

Sandora was a desert, for the most part, but a lot of the inhabited territory had so much agricultural boon that it almost seemed impossible. I wondered if this was the work of nature spirits, contradicting the natural environment.

There were split opinions on what had happened to Sandora. Some viewed it as a heroic act that freed the slaves, while others viewed it as the work of a demon that had crushed a country.

I wasn't too surprised to hear stories had grown to that extent, hyperbole was just another fact of life, after all. But one of the rumors said that I had destroyed that one city the wicked god ended up consuming...

It was true that I'd burned it to the ground, but that was more a cremation than anything.

Either way, it wasn't as bad as the Yulong rumors, so I wasn't too irritated. But there were still people out there who thought I was the source of the Phrase invasion... I couldn't see why they'd think that. Those things are a pain in the ass to everyone.

I decided to focus on the current emergency, I needed help from the other world leaders, pronto. I opened up an app on my smartphone...

By the end of it all, we had four-hundred-and-twelve Frame Gears lined up in the desert. They belonged to the following nations:

The Kingdom of Belfast
The Refreese Imperium
The Kingdom of Mismede
The Regulus Empire
The Ramissh Theocracy
The Roadmare Union
The Kingdom of Lihnea
The Kingdom of Palouf
The Knight Kingdom of Lestia
The Demon Kingdom of Xenoahs
The Magic Kingdom of Felsen

Each nation had three Knight Barons and twenty-seven Chevaliers, a total of thirty each.

Brunhild had its nine Valkyries, the three commanding units (Shining Count, Knight Baron, and Blue Moon), and seventy Chevaliers.

Assuming ten-thousand Phrase appeared, that meant each Frame Gear needed to kill about twenty-four enemies. I anticipated that the majority of the creatures would just be small-fry, Lesser Constructs, but I couldn't be sure until they appeared. We needed to take care not to be swarmed, though.

"This heat really sucks. Only the custom Frame Gears have cooling functions added... It's fine while the hatch is open, but once we get fighting it'll be a bit of a pain."

"I hope they appear at night, then."

"If that happens we'll have low visibility." The knight king of Lestia and the king of Lihnea replied to my complaining. It was probably annoying when we had to fight at night in the past. I didn't know for sure because I passed out after killing Gila during the last night battle.

Frame Gears were coated with protective paint that meant they wouldn't get so hot you could fry an egg on them, but it would still become stuffy and uncomfortable in the cockpit.

"We've prepared plenty of water, so don't get dehydrated out there. And be mindful of the terrain, too. There's a possibility of losing your footing, so I'd recommend you all try to move a bit before the fight starts." There was the possibility of death if the Frame Gears fell, after all. We did have an emergency protocol that I'd programmed into the Frame Gears, one that teleported people away from their mechs after enough damage was sustained...

But if the cockpit itself was crushed too quickly, it wouldn't have enough time to activate.

The Phrase were targeting human heartbeats, so it stood to reason they might just directly go for the cockpits.

We'd set up a ramshackle command center in the middle of the desert. It was built out of several shipping container-like structures, all joined together with a central tent. The world leaders were all in here, checking over their plans in conjunction with the map spread across the central table.

We'd used magic to keep the command center nice and cool, but leaving the safety bubble caused things to get very hot, very fast.

"We'll likely get an Upper Construct, right?"

"Like the one that destroyed Yulong's capital? I'd like to avoid seeing one, if possible..." The doge of Roadmare and the overlord both murmured to each other as they watched the live video feeds of the desert outside.

"I don't think we'll see one this time. I think it'll mostly just be Lesser and Intermediate Constructs. There might be some metal devils, though…"

"You mean the golden ones?"

"Yes. They're only slightly stronger than regular Phrase to start, but they can feast on their former kin to become even stronger. If we see any, make them the primary targets." I didn't know for sure if they'd appear, but it was better to be safe than sorry. I was personally more worried that another Dominant Construct could appear.

We also had an emergency escape route in place within the command center, it was a portal we could run through to escape back to Brunhild in a worst-case scenario.

Lapis came walking through that very portal, bringing a meal for everyone within the building. It was lunchtime.

The Frame Gear pilots all got rice balls, a flask of fresh water, and some bite-sized sandwiches. The world leaders, on the other hand, got some chilled ramen.

Chilled ramen was a specialty from the Yamagata prefecture. It was much like regular ramen, but it was cooled down and didn't have as much congealed fat or oil. The soup and the noodles were entirely cold.

It wasn't sour like chilled Chinese noodles, and it was the kind of thing that just made you wanna keep eating it. I once visited relatives in Yamagata and basically became a chilled ramen addict as a result.

The soup was good, it had plenty of soy sauce in it. The noodles were nice and stretchy, and it had sliced chicken, a boiled egg, menma, narutomaki, and green onions alongside it. There were lots of peppers, too.

"Ohoho… I've never had this before, but it is rather refreshing."

"Ahh... The meat's so tender... I love it!" The other world leaders seemed to enjoy it. I made a mental note to pass on their compliments to Crea later on.

Given that the world leaders had spent their lunches eating in Brunhild after our monthly conferences, they were all accustomed to eating with chopsticks. The new members from Felsen, Xenoahs, and Palouf were still using forks, though.

"Oh, that reminds me... Grand Duke. Will you be sharing the Phrasium fragments with us this time around?" The king of Felsen spoke up as he slurped his ramen. He was probably thinking about how much purer Phrasium chunks were than spellstones. It would be a golden chance for Felsen to get their hands on some. He likely wanted to incorporate them into the magic train development.

"Yeah, sounds fine. We'll ask for a cut since you're renting the Frame Gears from us, but everything else you guys can divide up and split." If the Frame Gears were damaged, I expected them to pay up in raw materials. They'd only have to pay the material needed to cover the repairs, though. Our workshop was fully automated, meaning there were no labor fees... But that was a national secret.

Yumina and the girls took it in turns coming into the command center to enjoy some ramen, too. It ended up being quite the hit dish. I ended up giving the chilled ramen recipe to the other world leaders, so they could enjoy it themselves.

The heat outside only intensified as the day went on. Monsters that nested in the desert sands also emerged from time to time. They weren't a match for our Frame Gears... Unless you counted the Sand Crawlers, they were huge and a pain in the ass. Either way, we decided not to engage them unless they engaged us.

I found myself quietly hoping the Phrase would just appear so I could go home and rest.

I left the tent and looked across the desert. But nothing happened. *Typical. They appear when I don't want them to, and stay away when I want them to show up.*

I took a step into the desert and suddenly saw something flicker in the corner of my eye.

"…Hm?" I felt a sudden presence about three meters in front of me. I didn't necessarily feel any hostility, I just felt something was there.

I imbued my eyes with divinity and surveyed the area. It was then that I noticed the sandy-looking Slime at my feet. It had a single large eye, which fixated on me once it realized I could see it. It stopped moving.

"…Just what are you, then? Some kind of monster?" It didn't exactly feel hostile. Even if it was a monster, I didn't plan on killing it if it wasn't going to attack me. I just wondered what it was. First I thought perhaps it could disguise itself like a chameleon, but it clearly only became visible once I employed divinity.

As I kept on staring at it, it slowly began to tremble.

Hmm…?

"Forgive this little one, please…" I suddenly heard the voice of a woman and turned my gaze away from the Slime.

The sand next to the little Slime began to twist and contort until it took the form of a woman with long, raven hair. Her skin was a dark tan, and she wore a simple cloth. There was also a faint light that shone around her body. *I know this feeling…*

"…You're a spirit?"

"I am, yes. I am the Sand Spirit that dwells within this desert. This child is one of my children, and it is so meek that it couldn't possibly pose a threat to you… That's why I beg you forgive it."

"Forgive it...? It didn't do anything to me, so it's not like I'm doing anything to it."

"Your gaze is imbued with divine power, so it cannot move an inch. The power of a god is absolute to spirits and their dependents. I assumed you were holding it in place as if to pass judgment." *Oh... I remember something like that, god did mention spirits in his sermon... Something about them helping gods by making the core parts of the world.*

I weakened my own divinity until the little Slime could move again. It slowly scampered behind the spirit, shivering behind her as if terrified. I felt pretty sorry for it.

"Mochizuki Touya... You've certainly been the subject of many rumors as of late."

"Really?"

"Indeed. The Wind Spirit. She likes to gossip and spread rumors, so they even managed to reach this place."

Huh, is the Wind Spirit a woman, then? Or maybe sex isn't really a thing since they're elemental essences... Guess it's just gender identity.

But man... The Wind Spirit is a gossip, huh? I guess it makes sense, what with rumors being carried on the wind and all that.

"Is there a reason you're all in the desert today?"

The Sand Spirit gestured toward the Frame Gears.

I figured I owed her an explanation, so I gave her the general gist. She was the Sand Spirit, which meant that she had dominion over this desert... It wouldn't be proper for us to cause chaos in her domain.

"You don't need to worry about explaining yourself. I was only a little curious."

"Thanks, then... I'm sorry for the trouble, we'll be done here after today."

"Worry not. This world belongs to those who dwell above the ground. We spirits merely watch over things and offer aid when we are needed. Well, not all spirits act the same... Some take a more active approach, while others don't really mind at all."

The Sand Spirit was more the latter type. She didn't really seem too concerned with human affairs, while the Wind Spirit sounded like she was a little too invested.

The Forest Spirit I'd met some time ago seemed to be the type that watched over people.

"Well, regardless... I wish you fortune in your coming battle. May we meet again." The Sand Spirit then melted back into the sand and vanished. The little Sand Slime bowed, or at least that's what it looked like, before joining its master in the sand. *Huh, that went pretty well. Her personality felt a little dry, though... Or maybe she's just dry because she's made of sand. Oh, that's right... I guess that means I can see spirits if I use my divine sight... Wonder if I'll be able to see the Wind Spirit if I use it.*

I looked up toward the sky and saw dozens of fairy-like creatures floating along the breeze. *Huh... Those aren't spirits. Maybe they're the dependents of the spirit, though.* The little dancing fairies didn't seem to notice us from so high up in the air, but it wouldn't have really mattered if they did or not.

I canceled my divinity and found my eyes were all dried out and uncomfortable... *Augh... they're all dry, ow... I'll have to get Flora to make me some eyedrops.*

"Oh, there you were, Touya."

I turned around to see Moroha and Karina standing nearby.

...Huh. You guys must've come through from Brunhild... But why?

Oh... Don't tell me... Yeah, I already know.

"...You want to join in the fight, right?"

"Ayup."

"Duh."

"Right..." It was useless to resist. The god of swords and the god of the hunt were both brimming with excitement, after all. It'd be fine so long as they held back from using their divinity, but if they ended up smashing the Phrase with ease then it'd defeat the whole point of bringing the Frame Gears out here to begin with... Either way, I didn't say anything. It wasn't my place.

"I know Moroha fights fine... But what about you, Karina? Are you planning on using a bow and arrow against them?"

"Don't underestimate me, kiddo. I don't just use bows, you know! I have spears, daggers, hatchets, and even guns at my disposal! I can use any tool used for hunting... To an extent. I'm not exactly a match for our dear god here."

Wow, really? Although I guess I remember seeing her spearfishing not too long ago...

"So give me a good weapon, alright?"

"...You're certainly not the god of subtlety, huh." I sighed as I opened up [Storage] and took out several Phrasium fragments. I fashioned them into a large spear. The blade itself was about the length of a regular shortsword's, attached to a long pole.

I'd reduced its weight a bit, but making it too light would make it awkward to handle.

Apparently, Karina didn't mind it being heavy, though. She was waving it around like a madwoman. The heavier it was, the better it was to smash stuff, so I didn't bother adjusting it anymore.

"It's a little fun to fight, even if we're holding back our divinity. It's not like we could do much fighting in the Divine Realm."

"It doesn't really look like you're holding back from here..."

"The humans of the world could reach this level given enough time and effort! It's not my fault they haven't set their minds toward taking advantage of their natural blessings."

"Is that right..." I didn't know whether to be amazed by her or if I should have just shook my head at her. I think if a human in this world "set their mind" toward reaching her kind of strength, they'd cease being human.

As I looked at the two and their ridiculous feats, I realized the slight hypocrisy in my words... After all, I wasn't exactly a regular human anymore, either.

Just as I thought that, the headquarters siren started blaring and a voice came over the loudspeakers.

"They've arrived!" I used [**Long Sense**] to project my sight ahead into the desert.

I saw a crack in space, shimmering in the desert heat. The crack opened up wide, splitting the sky down the middle. Phrase began to pour forth from the hole, endlessly. They were all Lesser and Intermediate Constructs.

"The Phrase have emerged! Mobilize the Frame Gears! Prepare for battle!" I yelled orders through my smartphone. I then took out two large Phrasium greatswords from [**Storage**] and passed them to Moroha. Then I used [**Fly**] to get an aerial grasp on the situation.

"Wait...!" I saw another crack in space not far away from the first one. From it poured several muddy-gold Phrase mutants. The metal devils were here.

There weren't as many of them as there were regular Phrase, but there were still more than I expected. *Of course... Of course these things had to show up, too...*

"This is bad… We don't want these things absorbing the others and getting out of hand." The mutants would consume the regular ones to increase their own strength. A Lesser Construct could probably turn itself into an Intermediate if it ate enough of its peers. I didn't even want to think of the possibility of a metal devil absorbing enough to become an Upper Construct… We had to prevent that.

"The mutants are here. All Valkyries roll out. Try to prevent them from getting near the regular Phrase."

Predicting the Phrase actions was harder now that the metal devils were involved.

We set up our camp directly between the emergence point and the nearest human settlement. The Phrase chased after heartbeats, so we figured standing in front of the nearest source would mean they'd come right to us.

Unfortunately, the presence of the mutants caused the regular ones to move erratically out of fear. We wouldn't be able to carry out the ambush now.

Luckily we had a strategy in place.

"Formation changing. Prepare for teleportation." Each and every Frame Gear suddenly materialized out of thin air, surrounding the Phrase in four directions. The new plan was to box them in and prevent escape.

Still, even with this kind of formation, it was possible that the combat would be more focused in some areas and quieter in other areas. I had no choice but to watch over the battlefield from above and give out orders.

The combat had begun in one corner. Elze and the girls began to make their move toward the mutants.

"The Phrase count is as follows: Ten-thousand-nine-hundred-and-fifty-four Lesser Constructs. Two-thousand-three-hundred-and-fifty-two Intermediate Constructs. Three-thousand-and-twenty-one Mutated Constructs." I heard Cesca's voice from my smartphone. *Good intel... Mutated Constructs is a pretty good designation.*

But damn it, there are way more than I thought. There were only around thirteen thousand during the Yulong situation. But whatever, so long as there are no Upper Constructs this should still be a cakewalk...

"Master. Detecting massive vibrations in hyperspace readings. An Upper Construct is emerging."

"Oh come on!" *We didn't get any readings indicating that, gimme a break! This isn't fair, there are too many as it is!* I saw space begin to crack open again, and an enormous crystal monster emerged.

It had a sharp beak, a long neck, two thick legs, and feather-shaped plumes coming up from its rear. It flapped its mighty wings. This was a bird-shaped Phrase... But no matter how I looked at it, it was just way too big.

The Phrase unfolded its long wings and shook its rear, unfurling its tail "feathers" like a paper fan. The sunlight rained down upon the display, causing it to glimmer.

"It's a goddamn giant peacock?!" I was amused by the fact that it had feathers that were clearly not feathers, but it wasn't the right time to focus on something like that.

Man, this is really bad... I guess I should send Elze and half of the others to deal with this while the others mop up the Mutated Constructs.

"Master. I'm detecting another massive vibration. A second Upper Construct is emerging."

"You what?!" I looked back over to the peacock and then scanned the battlefield until my eyes fell on another crack on the opposite side of the battlefield.

The second Upper Construct shattered itself through space in much the same way as the first.

This one looked pretty disgusting. It looked just like a nautilus. It had a coiled, ammonite-like shell, and stretched out countless massive feelers.

Several spikes protruded from its coarse crystal shell.

"This is getting ridiculous! Now there are two of them?!" I stared down at the battlefield, unable to figure out our next course of action.

The Nautilus Phrase floated about four meters in the air above the desert sand. My grandfather told me that nautiluses gathered gas in their shells and expelled it regularly, causing them to bob up and down as they floated through the water.

Apparently, this motion reminded the novelist Jules Verne of a submersible vehicle, which is why he named the submarine in his novel after the creature.

At the very least, the nautiluses on Earth weren't capable of swift movements, but it wasn't like the same rules would apply here.

"What do we do... I didn't expect to see two come up... Can we even beat two at the same time? Is that even possible?" I did have my trump card in place. We had our special cannon, the Brionac, that could fire out drilling bullets. A good shot from that would be able to take out an Upper Construct with little effort.

But it would still take time to line up a shot, so we couldn't do any hits in quick succession. Plus we'd need to disassemble it and build it back up before we could line up the second shot on the other Upper Construct.

Not to mention the fact that vast quantities of magic power, specifically wind and fire, were required to fire off a shot.

It'd be fine if I did it, but with my newfound divinity, there was a chance I could overload the machine and blow it up like I did with the Dverg. If that happened, then Linze and Leen would be in danger since they'd be the ones holding it. That's why I was hesitant to use it.

I couldn't even use [Slip] since we were fighting in desert terrain. The winds would just scatter the sand before it could be effective.

"I guess there's nothing else for it... Meteor Rain!" In the sky above the two Upper Constructs, several softball-sized chunks of Phrasium appeared one after the other. They began to fall down like shooting stars thanks to the magic weight enhancement I'd given them.

The peacock raised its head as if noticing the incoming barrage.

Suddenly a high-pitched noise rang out through the battlefield. The peacock spread its tail feathers and aimed them skyward. There were round patterns on the tips of the feathers that resembled focused lenses. I saw small lights gathering on each feather, and I really didn't like where the situation was headed. In a flash, several lasers fired out of the feather parts. They shot down the incoming projectiles. Or rather, they simply obliterated them.

What the hell! That's like a scattershot with the power of a railgun! How am I meant to go up against that?! I looked on in despair as the Peacock Phrase folded its feathers back, and returned them to their folded position as if holstering its weapon.

Why'd it do that? Does it need to recharge like the Brionac? Either way, that scattershot is bad news... We need to take this one out fast! "Monica! Call down the Brionac from the hangar immediately! Linze, Leen, get ready to fire!" I yelled into my smartphone.

I had enough ammo in my [Storage] for another Meteor Rain, but only enough for one more go. It definitely wouldn't be enough to kill the Upper Construct.

That's why the new plan was to use Meteor Rain as we charge up the Brionac shot. Then we'd be able to hit it with the Brionac shot after it wastes its next attack on the projectiles.

The issue was simply holding out until then…

The Brionac Cannon came down from Babylon, and it was then secured by Grimgerde and Helmwige.

The two Frame Gears linked themselves to Brionac via a cord in their backs, and then the cannon itself was anchored into the sandy ground.

"Brionac connected! Commencing charge!" Linze's voice was accompanied by a slow filling meter on the side of the cannon. I checked on it as I sent orders to the other Valkyries.

"Elze, Yae, Hilde! Distract the Peacock Phrase and keep its attention away from Leen and Linze! Lu, Yumina, keep the Nautilus Phrase away from the Peacock! Sakura, Sue, you two defend Leen and Linze. Forget about the mutants for now!" I was concerned that the Nautilus might have a laser as well. The Meteor Rain would be rendered useless if that thing ended up firing it off as well.

The Mutants were a pain, but the Chevaliers were still capable of taking them out. They were probably gonna go for the regular Phrase before us, anyway.

"Gah… These feathery parts keep getting in the way!" Elze gradually approached the Peacock Phase, but it kept swiping its tail feathers toward her.

Yae and Hilde were hot on Elze's heels, dashing toward the beast while avoiding its swipes.

The three of them arrived at its right leg at around the same time, and the three of them immediately went on the offensive.

"Take thiiis! Crusher!"

"Kokonoe Secret Style: Phoenix Cutter!"

"Lestian Sacred Sword: Iron Slice!" Gerhilde's Pile Bunker, Schwertleite's katana, and Siegrune's greatsword all struck the leg at the same time.

The Peacock Phrase had much thinner legs than any of the Upper Constructs we'd seen so far. It was unable to bear the combined strikes and immediately shattered.

"Woohoo!" The Peacock quickly lost its balance, causing the three Frame Gears to flee as it fell to the ground.

The impact on the desert sands kicked up a dust storm in the vicinity. Unfortunately, it regenerated its leg immediately... But we'd still bought a few precious moments.

Lu's Waltraute was currently equipped with its Booster Unit, running rings around the Nautilus Phrase as she caught its attention.

It slowly bobbed through the air, launching its tentacles out like spearing projectiles. Lu's B-Unit allowed insane speed, however, meaning she dodged each impact with ease.

The Nautilus definitely wasn't as fast as the Peacock. It wasn't even flying, it was just kind of lazily bobbing up and down in the air.

Either way, we couldn't afford to lower our guards. Even if its body was slow, its tentacles were moving at quite intense speed. If the Waltraute wasn't equipped with its B-Unit, Lu probably wouldn't have been able to avoid them so easily.

I suddenly heard a ringing noise followed by a loud crash, one of the tentacles fell to the ground. Yumina had managed to snipe one with Brunnhilde's gun.

Or at least that's what I assumed. Brunnhilde was completely cloaked, making it hard to see. If the stealth mode was deactivated, the sunlight would bounce right off its silver exterior and blind everyone nearby...

"The cannon's full! We can fire off!" Leen's communication came through, causing me to look back at the Peacock.

It was starting to stand back up.

It seemed to have noticed the Brionac cannon, which was pointed right at it. It spread its wings out and started firing surfboard-shaped crystal feather projectiles toward Leen and Linze.

The feathers fired with intense speed, but Sue appeared out of nowhere in her Ortlinde. It had activated its Overlord mode and stood tall.

"Stardust Shell!" The great mech held its left hand up and formed a defensive barrier. All the incoming missiles thudded against it before falling to the ground.

When it came to defense, Ortlinde just couldn't be beaten. Sue was the youngest, after all, so I made sure her Frame Gear could never get her hurt.

The feathers began to regenerate on the Peacock Phrase, and I saw my golden opportunity.

"Let's finish this... Meteor Rain!"

This time the projectiles fell down solely toward the Peacock Phrase. It spread out its tail and began to prepare its interception attack.

Just like before, the lasers scattered out and took care of the incoming attack, but that's exactly what I was waiting for.

"Do it!" Helmwige and Grimgerde activated the Brionac on my command, sending out the massive bullet with a mighty roar.

The drill bullet kicked up dust and sand as it flew straight ahead toward its target.

It impacted the Peacock Phrase's body and began to work its way inside. Eventually, it drilled its way through the orange core in the middle of the creature's chest and smashed its way out the back.

The Peacock Phrase stopped moving entirely, and cracks began to course through its form. In a matter of seconds, it screeched and collapsed into crystal debris, leaving nothing behind but a mountain of Phrasium.

"That's one down!" I turned to see steam rising from Brionac, Grimgerde, and Helmwige.

"You two okay?"

"I-I'm okay, yes… No problems."

"I'm quite okay… Somehow. My magic is almost completely spent, however…" I sighed in relief, knowing that their engagement rings would be able to replenish their exhausted mana pools at least a little.

Still, the physical fatigue from suddenly draining their reserves wasn't so easily mitigated. Physical strength was necessary to keep going while you were running on empty, after all. Firing the Brionac took a lot out of them, so they still needed their rest.

Helmwige and Grimgerde were also damaged due to the recoil, so they wouldn't be able to do much going forward.

"I'll have you both warp back to the base immediately. Flora will help you out, okay?" It wasn't just Rosetta who was standing by at HQ, Flora was also there to treat the injured combatants who were sent back.

I opened up a [Gate], sending the girls back to base along with Brionac and their Frame Gears.

Only the Nautilus was left.

"Touya!" I suddenly turned around at Yumina's exclamation. What I saw shocked me. The Nautilus Phrase was still bobbing up and down in the air, but several of the metal devils were clinging to its body.

They were gradually wearing away at the creature, as if melding their own bodies to it, partially melting themselves in the process.

It continued to struggle against them, using its tentacles to swipe them to bits, but they had the advantage of a swarm.

There were just way too many for it to deal with. The Nautilus Phrase's body was slowly dyed a muddy gold as more and more of the Mutated Constructs melded into it, ultimately converting it to their species.

Eventually, it fell to its side, screeching loudly as its tentacles lashed out at random targets.

...They're not eating it... They're converting it!

"T-Touya-dono, look at that!" Several gnarled spines began to grow from the Nautilus' shell, and its thin tendrils bulked out and became squid-like tentacles.

Its body was transforming. It had a metallic sheen to it now and was completely muddy-gold. Its entire body seemed more angular, ominous, and sharp.

The Nautilus began to move erratically, slowly, and rose up.

It was wrong to even call it a Nautilus at this point. It had taken on a disturbing new form, like a cross between a squid, an octopus, and a snail.

Its body seemed a lot larger, too. It must have grown in proportion to the number of Mutated Constructs that invaded its body.

It wasn't done shifting its form, though... Gradually as it contorted, its shell split down the middle, exposing several sharp, thorn-like protrusions.

It suddenly began firing those protrusions off in several directions, blasting them like rockets. They exploded in the air like fireworks, resulting in a rain of small, sharp debris that began to pelt the desert sand.

"[Shield]!" I managed to block the sudden downpour with magic.

The clustered attack reminded me of the fight against the Crocodile Phrase in Yulong.

The attack was indiscriminate, aiming for friend and foe alike. The debris rained down on Phrase and Frame Gears both. The Upper Construct had been converted to the side of the mutants, so it was no longer affiliated with the regular Phrase.

I looked around the battlefield and saw several Lesser Constructs break apart as they were impacted, I also saw several Frame Gears lose limbs. The Phrase would be able to regenerate so long as their cores were intact, but our soldiers weren't so lucky.

"Rosetta! Give me a damage report!"

"Twenty-nine Frame Gears received considerable damage, sir! Seven were obliterated, sir! Fortunately, all seven pilots were recovered safely. Two of the pilots have been critically wounded, however. They won't die, but they will need serious medical attention!" *Shit, they must've been hit in the cockpit... At least they're not dead.*

"Touya! Look out!"

"Huh?!" I turned my head to the sound of Lu's voice and saw the Mutated Upper Construct prepare another volley.

It launched its spiny missiles again, scattering the crystal debris throughout the desert. *Knock it off, you bastard!* Nineteen units were badly damaged, and eight more were taken out of commission. Three more men were severely injured, and could no longer take part in the battle. If this kept up, we'd be in major trouble...

"Touya, you hear me?"

"Doc?" A sudden transmission came from Doctor Babylon. I wondered what she wanted at a time like this. "It doesn't exactly have all the kinks worked out, but I don't think you care about that. I'm sending your Frame Gear down there!"

"What?! It's finished?!"

"More or less… Around ninety percent. You won't be able to use it to its full potential, but it's ready to be piloted." Particles of light began to form into the desert before they scattered to reveal my very own Frame Gear.

The body was coated in Phrasium armor, and golden veins ran through its transparent parts. It was around the same size as a regular Frame Gear. It had something on its back that looked like folded wings, but they were actually part of its support equipment.

It had a katana at each waist side, leaving no room for a shield. It was an offensively-oriented Frame Gear, after all… Two mighty horns protruded from its head, giving it an intimidating aura.

This was my Frame Gear, the multi-purpose combat mech, Reginleif.

Gleaming in the desert sun, my very own war machine stood tall. Seeing it like that made me believe it was truly worthy of its secondary title, "The Successor of the Gods."

I was almost moved to tears by the sight of my long-awaited Frame Gear, but I had no time to lose.

I flew through the sky and opened up the cockpit. I sat down in the hatch and closed it, while savoring that new-mech smell. I placed my smartphone down on the console in front of me.

A low rumble began to emanate as the various gauges and meters inside Reginleif began to come alive. The wide monitor turned on, showing me a broad field of vision. It wasn't a three-sixty degree view, but it was close.

I grabbed the control stick in front of me and began to channel my magic through it. Reginleif turned its head as if to answer my call. It was completely synced up with my intentions.

Taking on an Upper Construct alone was no simple feat... But I had faith in my new ally.

"Alright, let's go then... Fragarach... Activate!"

"Initializing Fragarach System." My smartphone spoke back as the wing-like structures on Reginleif's back unfolded themselves and broke off until they orbited my mech. There were now a total of twelve crystal slabs surrounding the machine.

"Switch to Sphere Mode."

"Recalibrating Fragarach... Sphere Mode activated." The slabs immediately turned into orbs, floating around Reginleif like satellites. This was thanks to the power of my [Program] and [Modeling] spells. It could easily shift modes, much like my Brunhild gun.

Alright, then... This seems good to me.

"Go get him!" The twelve crystal orbs blasted toward the Mutated Upper Construct. It transformed several of its appendages into blade-like limbs and tried to cut them down, but the spheres simply smashed right into them and left them shattered. They then pelted its muddy-gold body.

Each of the Fragarach Spheres was over a meter in diameter, and I'd applied [Gravity] in order to make them far heavier than they had any right to be. They weren't as powerful as a shot from the Brionac, but it could easily obliterate most Phrase structures.

The grotesque mutant floated in the air as it continued to receive a pounding from all twelve spheres. It was like watching a suspended punching bag being knocked around by a boxer. Its body was dented and crumpled, kind of like a car after a bad accident.

"Switch to Blade Mode."

"Recalibrating Fragarach... Blade Mode activated." The crystal spheres immediately reformed into blades. They began to dance through the air, slicing freely at the Mutated Upper Construct's limbs.

While it was distracted, I took the opportunity to spear its body with half of the Fragarachs. They weren't able to reach its core, however. Due to its muddy-gold body, it was harder to see where the core actually was.

"If that's how you wanna play it, fine!" I called all the Fragarachs back, converted them into their base forms.

"Switch to Lance Mode!" The twelve crystal slabs all began sliding into each other until they formed a massive lance.

Reginleif grasped it and leaped into the sky before flying toward the Mutated Upper Construct. Unlike Linze's Helmwige, Reginleif didn't need to transform to become airborne. It was capable of using [Fly] as an extension of myself.

"[Accel]!" With a single word, my speed boost caused Reginleif to blast forward at supersonic speed, driving the lance into my foe. The mech charged forward faster than a speeding bullet, pushing the lance tip through the creature fully, impaling it entirely. Its body began to splinter and crack, before falling to pieces.

I looked at the golden fragments until I finally found its blood-red core.

"Switch to Blade Mode!" The lance in my hand changed into twelve separate blades, and immediately they ran themselves through the core.

A crack ran through the middle, and the core shattered into pieces.

After a few moments, the metallic shards of the Mutated Upper Construct melted into goop.

I was already high above the ground at that point, gazing down at the liquid as it seeped into the sand.

Reginleif was unlike any other Frame Gear I'd ever handled... It moved just like an extension of my own body.

"What a display... How was it, Touya?"

"Incredible, Doc... Really incredible."

"Wonderful! That's to be expected, though... It has all the features of the other Valkyries and more. I even included something that'll surprise you."

"...It isn't a self-destruct feature, is it?"

"I'll admit I thought of implementing something like that, but I canceled it. It would be a waste to destroy my masterpiece." *That's your reason? How about having a little consideration for me?! I'm the pilot!*

Either way, the Mutated Upper Construct was finished. All we had to do was mop up the rest of the battlefield.

I brought up my monitor and had it display the remaining enemies. There were a lot to the north and east. My sisters were headed eastward... So I decided to head north.

The Fragarachs changed back into their slab forms and docked back on to Reginleif's back, giving it its winged appearance once more.

"Yumina... Could you and the other Valkyries take care of the mutants? I'll handle the Phrase in the northern area."

"Copy that. Please take care."

"Mhm." I had Reginleif give the girls a thumbs-up before taking it through the air toward the northern part of the desert.

As I got closer, I noticed that the Frame Gears under the control of Lihnea and Palouf were the ones engaging the Phrase in this area.

The Paloufean knights weren't quite as talented as the Lihnean ones were, but they were trying their best to support. Still, they were clearly overwhelmed in terms of numbers.

I saw a prone Paloufean Frame Gear about to be blasted by a laser-firing Mantis Phrase.

"Switch to Reflector Mode." The twelve crystal slabs quickly slid off Reginleif's back and immediately formed a wall in front of the fallen Frame Gear.

The laser hit the wall of Fragarachs, bouncing it off at a random angle into the sky. If the attacker hadn't been a Phrase, I would've just directed the laser right back at them.

I unsheathed a katana and used it to cleave the Mantis Phrase in half with a single strike. I didn't even have to aim to take out its core, it was laughable.

"Switch to Dagger Mode." The wall of Fragarachs split back into twelve pieces, and then each piece split into four. The small pieces then turned into pointed, dagger-like objects. This mode effectively turned twelve slabs into forty-eight daggers.

The daggers began to orbit around Reginleif.

Let's do this!

"Gladius!" The forty-eight projectiles immediately broke out of orbit and descended to the battlefield below, penetrating Phrase cores over and over again. They glittered in the sunlight as they continued to hunt down their prey.

Gladius was the name I'd given to this attack, one that was ruthless, omnidirectional, and all at once.

Technically speaking, I have to manipulate the Fragarachs by myself. Even though there were support systems in place, I'd say my upper control limit would be about six swords. The more you try to control, the sloppier your control over them would become. In the worst case scenario, they'd start hitting each other, or things other than your targets.

However, Reginleif was an extension of myself and thus was subject to the accelerated mental processes that [**Accel**] granted me. Thanks to that, I could freely control all forty-eight blades at a time.

If I lost my focus, however, I could still miss. Originally I planned on using my smartphone's auto-target function, but I realized that it wouldn't let me change my motions on the fly, or react to situations effectively in real-time.

It was still cumbersome, though. Forty-eight definitely felt like overkill, too. Plus I had to take care not to become too focused on the weapons to the point where my control on the main mech became loose. Fortunately, this mode was just for big clean-up situations.

Lesser Constructs could easily be destroyed with just a single strike, but Intermediate Constructs required me to fuse four or so into a larger blade to pierce its defenses.

Before I even knew it, at least five-hundred Phrase died to my sudden attack.

I recalled the daggers, and they began orbiting Reginleif again like satellites.

"Whew…" I heard celebratory cheers coming from the nearby knights, but I just slumped back in my chair and let loose a relieved sigh.

Man… That was a little more stressful than I expected.

But it wasn't over, the battle was still raging elsewhere. I needed to support people in other areas of the Desert, too. I was about to move again when I heard the systems around me begin to power down. I wondered what the hell was happening. Even the lights on the dashboard in front of me were going off.

I continued to look around in confusion as my mech began to descend. Even the little daggers combined back into wings and quickly sat on Reginleif's back.

"What's going on here?!"

"Don't panic, Touya. You've simply gone beyond the Operational Limit."

"The what now?!" I glared in exasperation at my smartphone as Doctor Babylon spoke through it. *I wasn't told about this!* Reginleif finished descending. It took a knee in the desert, so I manually opened the cockpit hatch. I immediately regretted my decision, as the desert heat was almost suffocating.

"Reginleif doesn't work like the other Frame Gears. It moves by taking in your magic directly. However, it can't fully endure the depth of your mana pool, Touya. That's why we have the Operational Limit in place, to shut it down before it overloads like the Dverg did... Clearly, the system still needs fine-tuning."

"Oh come on..." It seemed like I couldn't use it for over ten minutes at a time. But that was a preferable alternative to having it detonate like the Dverg did... I definitely didn't want to be responsible for trashing the best Frame Gear we had.

Hmm... I wonder if we can make it run longer if we have it save some magic in reserve... But damn, what about the fight? Ah... Whatever, the others should be able to take it from here. I'm just glad I didn't hit the limit before defeating that big one.

The limit meant that Reginleif had to be more carefully considered in terms of timing. It was possible we could end up expecting an Upper Construct only to deploy Reginleif and have no Upper Construct appear at all.

It was possible that we could have a situation like this battle, where two appeared without warning... It'd be really bad if there was a long delay between when they emerged, too.

I took my smartphone from the console and hopped out of my cockpit on to Reginleif's shoulder. The sunlight was only intensifying, and it was uncomfortable.

"Man… Thank you, Reginleif. I'll be in your care going forward." I looked over my new partner with a smile on my face. *Oh crap, right… I should send the Paloufean and Lihnean Knights to fight in other areas.*

I gently placed Reginleif into **[Storage]**, then sent the waiting knights to another part of the battlefield.

"Well?"

"Their wavelengths have ceased transmission. Both have been terminated."

"Unfortunate. It must have been the same individual that destroyed Gila."

Two people stood talking to each other in the space between worlds. They didn't seem at all bothered by the fact that their surroundings were naught but a roaring void.

One was a young man. The other, a young woman. They looked similar to each other. At a glance, one might take them to be brother and sister. But this wasn't technically correct. They were, in a sense, clones. Fragments of the same self.

Even amongst the Dominant Constructs, they were anomalies. Twins that shared a single heart and origin.

Dominant Constructs are born as cores. After a long gestation period, accumulating experiences as a mindless entity, they awaken as an individual. Childhood is not something they really understand. Upon awakening, a Dominant Construct is merely itself, and that's all it knows.

Now and then, a Dominant Construct may be born with two cores. Ordinarily, they would continue their evolution and simply awaken as a mature form with two cores instead of one.

However, these two were a representation of an abnormal circumstance. During their gestation, the cores split and developed into separate individuals.

They each had long bangs that covered half of their face. The girl's hair covered her right eye, while the boy's covered his left. That meant that each of them only had a single, golden eye visible.

Their physical features were largely the same. Well, not entirely. The feminine one had somewhat of a softer physique, and her chest was a little more defined.

"Shall we go out to play next time the barrier rips, Leto?"

"I think not, Luto. It isn't our turn yet, after all. Yula will cause quite the ruckus if we leave." Though they were born at exactly the same time, the feminine one often treated the masculine one as a younger brother. Amusingly, the boy felt as though the girl was the younger one.

The girl was known as Leto, while the boy was known as Luto. They were clearly Dominant Constructs, but even at a glance, you could tell they were different.

Parts of their crystal bodies were dyed a muddy gold, after all. That mark was the evidence they had evolved to a level beyond that of a standard Dominant.

"Just how long must we wait here?" Luto turned around, facing the enormous egg-like cocoon behind them. Occasionally a beating sound would resonate from the throbbing sac, much like a pumping heart.

The two of them flinched slightly as they felt an oscillation in space.

"Oh? We have a visitor." Leto spoke into the dark void before him. Another Dominant Construct emerged from the black.

She had long, crystal hair, and deep crimson eyes. Her form was slender and tall. It was the creature known as Ney.

She was the leader of the faction that sought to recover the Sovereign.

She stared at the twins with fury blazing in her eyes.

"You little shits… Why did you send the Gilded out into that battle?!"

"I don't believe we owe you any explanation or notice, Ney. We're no longer allies, are we?" Leto giggled softly as if to mock the intruder. Luto smirked a little, as well.

"Unlike you, we no longer care about matters as trivial as the Sovereign Core. We can become strong without it, after all."

"I told you I'm not after the Sovereign's power, didn't I?!"

"Then why do you continue to cross worlds like this? Even if the new Sovereign was weak, they were still the leader, right? You should have stayed back on Phrasia and supported them."

"No!" Ney was unable to come up with a response. To Ney, there was no Sovereign other than the woman she knew. Accepting a new Sovereign would mean throwing away all her memories of the person she revered. She couldn't possibly do such a thing.

That's why she listened to Yula and crossed worlds using the method he'd created. It required the power of multiple Dominant Constructs to even attempt to travel from world to world, which is why even though they butted heads, none of them had attacked each other.

She knew that Yula and Gila were after the Sovereign Core, but she had to rely on their strength to keep chasing after it. The situation caused her to grit her teeth in frustration more than once or twice.

She was trying to bring the Sovereign back home, while Yula aimed to take the Sovereign's strength for himself. It was obvious that once they found the Sovereign Core, their alliance would turn into open hostility.

But then, out of nowhere, Yula suddenly began acting strangely. He'd obtained a strange new power and began creating new Phrase using it. The bizarre, gilded monsters that came out, as a result, could hardly be called kin to beings like Ney.

Yula's goal was now no longer focused on the Sovereign at all. By all accounts, this should've been something for Ney to celebrate, but she found a pit in her stomach as she saw her fellow Phrase eroded and converted into what she referred to as the Gilded.

"Well, whatever you wish to do with the Sovereign, it matters not to us. Yula doesn't really care either. But I do wonder… Will the golden cocoon hatch faster if we feed the Sovereign to it?"

"You bastard!"

Luto giggled like a madman, which made Ney storm toward him and throw a punch his way. Her hand was caught by Leto. The little one began to squeeze it hard.

"If I might be honest, Ney… I was rather irritated by your constant spiel about how great the Sovereign is. We're no longer allies… So it's fine if I do what I want to you, right? Would it be fine if Luto and I devoured you?" Leto grinned as she began to wear away at the woman's arm. Ney looked on in horror as she saw her own hand sink into Leto's body, it was already gone down to the wrist. She'd lost all feeling in her hand, and could no longer move it.

A filthy golden color began to crawl up Ney's arm. She quickly morphed her free hand into a blade and chopped it off before it could spread to her body any further.

She then jumped backward, attempting to put some distance between her and the others.

"Oh dear. Seems I missed my opportunity to eat all of you." Leto grinned broadly as she absorbed what remained of the severed arm. It melted into the younger Dominant Construct's body and vanished without a trace.

"Guh…" Ney regenerated her shattered arm and turned around, fleeing into the darkness of the void.

The power that Leto exhibited was one granted to her and her brother by Yula. It was known as Absolute Corrosion. The disgusting ability allowed them to take other Phrase into their bodies and absorb their power.

Not even Dominant Constructs were free from this power. One suffering from the affliction needed to sever the affected body parts immediately. If it reached their Core, everything would be over.

Even the thought of that Corrosion reaching her core was a borderline traumatic experience for Ney.

Luto attempted to give chase, but was stopped in his tracks by his sister.

"Leave her be. She has no power here. We simply need to remain and watch over the cocoon, as we were told."

"Tsk. How annoying. I'm bored here… I wonder if that fellow we encountered the other day will come here again." Luto sighed quietly and lay down on his back.

"Are you referring to Endymion?"

"Yes. We certainly managed to kill a lot of time by playing with him. Though… Given the state he was in by the end of it, I don't even know if he's alive anymore." Luto grinned as if recalling a fond memory. Even though he had said he didn't know, Leto was aware that Luto believed the badly beaten, half-dead man was still alive. There were no secrets between the two, for they were part of an originally intended whole.

They enjoyed the brief interaction with Ney, but nothing more seemed to be happening that day.

The two of them shrugged and sat next to each other, whiling away the hours, planning out how many Gilded Phrase to send to the other side next time a rip opened.

$$\diamond \quad \diamond \quad \diamond$$

"Hmm... This could be trouble..." In the Divine Realm, in a certain little room, the god of worlds groaned to himself as he watched the scene play out on his television set.

"I told you, pops! Isn't it already going a little too far? We need to pull the trigger on this situation before it spreads to even more worlds. Hell, you know what I'd do! I'd pull the plug on the whole situation!" The loud man leaned his elbow on the table behind the God Almighty, while loudly munching some cookies.

He was around sixty years and had a massive bulky body. His face was unshaven, his eyes were jet black, and his shaggy hair was equally raven. He took a sip from his tea and shoveled more cookies into his mouth.

"When you say pull the plug... You mean to destroy the world, do you not?"

"That's totally what I mean, pops! I'm the god of destruction, ain't I?" The man, or rather the god, laughed as he spoke without reservation.

There were various worlds maintained by various gods. Every now and then, a world might leave the protection of a god, and in that case, it's up to the god of destruction to obliterate thát world entirely.

Typically, divine powers were not used in mortal realms. Often at best they were used by lower-tier gods with limited power, or by dependents of gods that were granted some form of abilities. The god of destruction was another matter entirely. He used his divinity to wipe worlds from existence.

But unless there were serious circumstances at play, it was unusual for a world to lose its divine protection. That meant the god of destruction rarely got to do much at all.

The fact that he was even visiting the god of worlds meant that there were indeed serious circumstances at play.

"If this keeps up, this world is totally gonna be out of your control, pops. I don't really get to decide if that's an issue… But things should be easier if I end that world before it becomes a problem, right?"

"I understand what you are saying, but… I left Touya in charge of that world…"

"Touya? Oh, you mean that little kid you put under your protection? You sure something like this is okay for him? It's pretty out of his depth, I think." The god of destruction frowned a bit. The events going on in that world were about to become highly unstable. He felt it unfair to entrust something so erratic to a mere fledgling god, much less some complete newbie without any formal title.

"I believe it will be fine. If all goes well, I think there will be no need for you to use your powers… Even if that world ends up falling out of my control, it may well be okay."

"Seems like you trust that kid a lot, huh. Well, that's fine if you say so… But are you sure those two worlds are gonna be okay?" The god of destruction gestured toward the TV screen. There were two planets lined up on either side, like a mirror image. The line between them, however, seemed oddly distorted.

"There's a wicked god there, right?"

"You are correct. It consumed a servile god, this case is most unusual. Nothing like this has ever happened before, after all."

"A god eater, huh?" The god of destruction picked up a rice cracker and chomped down.

"This would usually be the time in which we create a Sacred Treasure, or send an Angel down there... But given it is the world I happened to send Touya to? I think he can handle it." The god of worlds sat down gently on his cushion.

"Seems like he's got quite the entourage, though. They didn't seem to mind descending down there."

"Probably because it is the first opportunity they've had for a vacation in tens of thousands of years. Even I enjoyed my trip down there."

"Oh, you did? Sounds like fun. Should I head down there, then?"

"Perish the thought. You and I both know that if you descended, the world would end." That wasn't a metaphor, either. If the god of destruction set foot down there, it would be a catastrophe.

"So that's it, then? You're gonna leave this problem to that Touya kid?"

"I am, yes. I will give up on it if he refuses to handle it, of course. He is much too unreliable as an actual god right now... But I think after two or three thousand years, he will turn out quite well."

"Well, hopefully he can handle that mess. I don't exactly relish killing all those people." The distortion between the two worlds was about to bring on unusual, potentially disastrous effects. The god of destruction firmly believed that obliterating both planets and establishing a hard reset was the best way to go about fixing it.

"Fine then, I'll wait before asking to destroy them again. But you should probably explain the situation to that kid."

"You are quite right... I will speak to him at some point, I promise. But I would like to keep an eye on the situation for the time being. It is still possible this distortion will vanish without our intervention."

"Are you sure about that?" They both knew that the chances of that happening were low. The god of destruction was fine for the time being, but he still believed forcing a hard reset was the optimal solution.

But he decided to trust God Almighty's intuition. Even though he was humanized, Touya was still one of the divine. He was around the level of an apprentice god. If he could focus himself, then things would be okay.

It wasn't uncommon for a god in human form to strike down wicked gods or evil Dragons, after all.

"How long's it been since a human became a god, anyway?"

"Hmm... Let me think... I don't quite recall. There are many humans and circumstances out there, after all. The chance to become a god is rather slim, as well."

"Heh... I've also never heard of anyone becoming a god by mistake... If you really did kill him by mistake, I mean..."

"That is quite enough speculation out of you, young man." God Almighty frowned at the god of destruction's nefarious grin.

It was certainly an unusual mistake, one he didn't quite understand making. But perhaps this too was the work of destiny, something beyond even a force as great as him. Either way, to the god of worlds, Mochizuki Touya was like a wonderful young grandson.

"Come to think of it, it's been a while since I saw the god of battle. You seen him?"

"If I remember correctly, he said something about having found a worthy apprentice..." The two gods continued their small talk around the table. On the TV screen in front of them, the distortion slowly began to transform into a whirlpool, as if something were close to emerging from the space between both worlds.

"This tastes great!" I chomped down a bite of food, then scooped up some rice and shoveled another bit of the pickled radish and yellowtail sushi into my mouth. It was really good...

The fatty fish really made me feel nostalgic. It was also the first time in a while I'd eaten such delicious daikon radish...

"How is it, Touya-dono? Do you like my mother's cooking, do you?"

"Yeah, I really do. This stuff's amazing, Yae..."

"Oh, my... I am pleased to hear that my food is fit for a world leader, I am... Thank you so much...!"

"Gahaha! Seems the young lord likes it a lot, honey!" Yae's mother, Nanae, was sitting opposite me and Yae. Her husband, Jubei, laughed heartily as he heard me compliment the food.

To be honest, this wasn't actually a yellowtail... But the fish was so close that it was practically the same thing as the one found on Earth. Besides, who really cared about getting the name right? It tasted too great to even worry about.

"This is tasty... I should be able to replicate this..." Lu sighed in relief as she sat next to me. She couldn't help but look at any dish with a chef's eye, it seemed.

We were visiting Eashen, since we hadn't been there in a while. Because of that, we were treated to a nice family meal in celebration of Yae's return home.

Other than Yae, we were joined by Lu, Hilde, and Sue. They all seemed equally impressed by Nanae's cooking.

"Would you like seconds?"

"Oh, thank you… If it's not too much trouble, I'll take some."

Ayane, who served the Kokonoe family as a housekeeper, took our empty bowls and promptly refilled them with side dishes and rice.

We had rice from Ieyahsu in Brunhild, so we could enjoy this kind of thing now and again. But it was definitely rare to enjoy home-cooked Japanese-style food like this, so I took the offer whenever I could.

I'd planned on going to meet with Ieyahsu to thank him for the rice he'd sent, but it seemed like he was busy in a meeting with the other Feudal Lords.

Yae's father was staying home for the day, but her older brother had to head straight to the castle and act as a bodyguard for the duration of the meeting.

After the incident with the servile god, the Tokugawa household established itself as the dominant power in Eashen. The other Feudal lords were basically treating him as the de-facto leader. It seemed like Ieyahsu had many busy days ahead of him.

Yae and Hilde headed to train in the dojo after they finished their food. She wanted to show the Lestian princess more of the Kokonoe style.

They also said exercising after a meal was a good habit to keep up, but I felt so full that I didn't really feel like moving… I was fine where I was.

I didn't need to do swordplay, so I decided to have some tea with Jubei. *Ah… This is nice, too…*

Lu and Sue went into the kitchen with Nanae to ask her about the food and help her wash up. *Ooh… Wonder if they're gonna make this back at Brunhild… Wait, we don't have any fresh yellowtail there… We could buy some, I guess?*

"Is my Yae doing alright over there?"

"She is. She trains with my knights, keeps public order in the castle town, and goes out hunting now and then. She's doing really well for herself."

"I was not the best of parents if I am honest… I trained my daughter and raised her to be a blade. But if that blade is something that keeps others safe, then I am a proud father." I didn't think Yae was just a blade. She was well respected in Brunhild, she cherished the people there, and her smile was something else. She respected her family, and the people she cared for. I honestly hoped that if I ever had a daughter, she'd grow up to be like Yae.

"In a few years I will be relinquishing my duties to my son, I will. Maybe I could retire to Brunhild and spend some time with my grandkids if I have any by then… Heh."

"…It might be a bit soon to be thinking about that… But maybe. You never know." I forced a smile back to Yae's father, but honestly, I just hoped that a peaceful future like that could come. The looming threat of the Phrase and the wicked god had me a little concerned.

After speaking a bit with Jubei, I decided to go outside and walk the streets of Oedo a bit.

"Touya! I'm coming too!"

Just as I was leaving the house with Kohaku, Sue came charging after me. Lu was still in the kitchen with Nanae. I hoped she didn't get too enthusiastic and wear herself out.

"Alright, let's go for a walk! C'mon!"

"Whoa!"

Sue suddenly grabbed my hand and jerked me forward. She'd grown a bit since we first met, and she was clearly a little stronger too.

We left the Kokonoe household and were greeted by the hustle and bustle of Oedo's streets.

There were people selling stuff on the streets. Cooked veggies, fresh fish, and even little bags with goldfish inside.

My mouth started watering when I caught a whiff of grilled eel, even though I'd just eaten.

"It's more crowded than Brunhild here."

"Well, that's just how it is. This is a pretty important city, after all." Oedo was the center of the Tokugawa territory, said to be the most bustling city in all of Eashen. Most of Eashen's culture originated within Oedo's walls, and many travelers came to visit it. It could be said that this city was the cutting edge of Eashenese culture.

There were still some foreigners here and there, but not really enough that you'd notice.

The two nations that bordered the sea across from Eashen were Horn and Nokia, and those countries were extremely isolated. Yulong didn't even exist anymore, either. Given all that, it wasn't too surprising to think that there wouldn't be many non-Eashenese people there.

I wasn't from Eashen, but I was a black-haired guy from Japan, and I basically resembled a native Eashenese person. Sue, however, prancing around in her fancy clothes with her long blonde hair... Definitely stood out. A sight like her was quite the rarity in a country like this.

Sue definitely knew that, but she didn't seem to mind. She wasn't self-conscious, at least.

Sue was the niece of a king, at the end of the day. She was probably used to getting attention from the public even back in Belfast.

"Touya, look! Dumplings! We should eat some!"

"Didn't we just eat?" Sue happily pointed me in the direction of a small tea shop. There was a small dining area outside, where a few patrons were enjoying tea and sweet dumplings.

There was a menu fixed on the wall nearby. It had almost all dessert items. It seemed to be more of a sweet shop than a tea shop. I personally didn't care much about eating anything for dessert, but I couldn't argue back against Sue. I took a seat with her and quietly resigned myself to fate, hoping I could get away with just having a cup of tea.

"Welcome. What would you like?"

"Uhm... I'll have a cup of tea, please. Sue, you wanted dumplings?"

"Mhm! I want mitarashi dango, yomogi dumplings, sesame-sprinkled ones... Ohh, and red bean paste! Oh... And zu... zuda mochi? I'd like that too, please!" *Whoa, calm down! That's way too much!* I made sure to specify to the waitress that we wanted small portions of each kind of dumpling she ordered. It would've been bad if we had a full order.

The tea came out right away. I was happy with my choice, it was delicious.

Sue was patient, so she waited until her tea cooled down. Kohaku also got water in a bowl.

"Sorry to keep you waiting."

"Ooh, that looks so cool!"

The plate came out with two little dumplings of each type. There were two green yomogi dumplings, two black sesame dumplings, two small red dumplings filled with bean paste, and two rice cakes with green paste on top. What Sue had referred to as zuda mochi was actually zunda mochi.

I was glad to see that it existed in Eashen, too. I ate that a lot with my late grandfather when I was a kid.

I got a little nostalgic, so I asked for a portion of my own. Sue had already started wolfing down her dumplings in the meantime. She seemed to find each one delicious... But she was definitely making a mess, she had sticky stuff all around her mouth.

As I reveled in Sue's soothing smile, some food for me arrived.

It looked great.

"Time for me to try it, then..." I picked up a bit with my chopsticks and popped it into my mouth. The taste of the edamame and the sweet fragrance tantalized my senses. It was a little different to the taste I remembered, but it was still amazing. Just like the fish I'd had earlier, even if it had a different name, it didn't stop the good taste.

"I want everyone to get a chance to try this..."

"Then let's take some home with us!" She was right, so I decided to do just that. I asked the waitress for a to-go order and placed the heavy box into [**Storage**].

As I leaned back and looked around, I caught a figure in the corner of my eye.

"......"

I could feel the burning stare of a small child not far away. She was about four or five years old, certainly smaller than Sue.

She looked like she was drooling as she held her finger up to her mouth, staring at the delicious food Sue was cramming into her face.

Sue herself was finished with her dumplings and moved on to the dango skewers, but it didn't take long for her to notice the girl.

"...Are you hungry?"

"Y-Yeah!" Sue asked a question as she held out a little bit of food and waved it toward the kid. The little girl came running over.

I couldn't possibly eat another bite, so I let her have the rest of my stuff.

"Is it good?"

"Mhm! Oedo food is really good!" The little girl was pretty strange, but she was hungrily devouring whatever we gave her. I wondered if she'd lost her parents. Looking at her more closely, there were a few odd details that stood out. To start with, she was wearing clothes that didn't match her size. Same with her shoes. If it was a size larger, it would be at risk of falling off her. The kimono she wore was also unusual. Her collar was untidy and her sash was tied a little too tight.

Her long black hair was glossy and clean, and there wasn't a single blemish on her skin. She looked pale, but she didn't exactly look malnourished.

I wondered what was up with her... She was a weird kid, for sure. "Uhm... I'm Touya. This is Sue. What's your name, and where do you come from?"

"Um... I'm Iroha! I'm from there!" She couldn't possibly be correct. The little girl pointed toward Oedo Castle, the massive towering structure in the middle of the city.

Huh? You're not one of Ieyahsu's kids, are you? No way... You don't look the part to be a noble... Are you sure about the castle being where you're from? Or are you just pointing at it as a landmark?

"What's your dad called?"

"Umm... To... Tojiro!"

Well, that rules out Ieyahsu. I was wondering if you were the kid of one of the Tokugawa concubines, but I guess not.

I sighed quietly and handed over a fresh set of chopsticks to Sue, who seemed like her sweet tooth wasn't quite sated.

"Thanks!"

"No problem." Sue started chowing down on some of the extra mochi. Her mouth was once again stained by syrup. I simply sighed and hoped she wouldn't spill any on her lap.

Iroha plucked up a bit of mochi before turning to us both.

"Where are you from mister?"

"Oh, I'm from Brunhild... It's a country far to the west. We're staying with a friend's family." We were actually staying with my fiancee's family, but I didn't want to complicate matters. Plus if I counted Jutaro as that friend, I wasn't really lying.

The zunda mochi was done with, but I could see on Iroha's face that she wasn't quite full. I ordered another portion.

"You're really nice, mister!"

"Of course he is. Touya's a truly good man! As expected of my husband, of course." *We're not married yet...* But I couldn't help but grin at Sue's goofy face.

I sat with the two of them, sipping at some more tea as they ate some more snacks... But then I heard a loud voice from nearby.

"Hey, over there! Found her!"

"Oh?!" I was just listening, when suddenly Iroha put down her plate and ran away as fast as she could. I didn't even have time to react.

"She ran for it! Chase her down!"

"Guh! She is not getting away this time!" Three men ran right past us in hot pursuit. The men were all dressed in black leather outfits. No matter how you looked at it, they were ninja.

I didn't know why I interfered, but I couldn't sense anything good in them chasing down a kid.

"[Slip]!"

"Gah!"

"Gwaugh!"

"Hgh!" The three men stumbled over their own feet and fell to the ground.

I paid my bill at the tea shop, boxed up the leftovers, and left the shop immediately.

I shoved the leftovers into **[Storage]** before pulling out my smartphone and running a search on the girl's location.

"Where'd she go?"

"She's heading toward Yae's dojo." I looked down at my phone to confirm the answer to Sue's question. Iroha seemed to have made it away safely. She was fast on her feet for such a little kid; Yae's place was quite a walk away from where we were.

As I checked my map, I headed toward a back alley.

《My liege, look at that girl.》

"Hm?" I looked over the street outside the alley and saw a young girl wearing an utterly gorgeous kimono. It was quite the opposite in looks to the one Iroha had been wearing... But the girl wearing it looked pretty suntanned and her hair was disheveled. Not to mention the fact that the outfit was a tiny bit too small for her, as well...

Wait, did Iroha maybe swap clothes with her? Sue went over to ask her where she got her kimono, and she answered that a young girl had exchanged clothing with her earlier.

"...Then does that mean Iroha was a noble after all?"

"If she's noble... Then she's gotta be in trouble, right? Why would a kid like her be chased down by ninjas?" I decided it'd be best to make sure she was safe. I had a fine enough level of control over **[Teleport]**, so I was confident I could jump straight to Iroha. It wasn't too far a distance, after all.

I grabbed Sue by the hand.

"[Teleport]!"

"Whoa!" We suddenly appeared directly in front of a surprised Iroha. There was nobody else around, she'd seemingly been hiding in a back street.

"Wh-Where did you come from?!"

"That's just Touya's power. Are you surprised? Pretty cool, huh?" Sue puffed out her chest as if to gloat. I had no idea what she was proud of, but her face was cute.

"Iroha… Why are you being chased down?"

"Oh! Th-They're bad guys! They keep getting in my way!" *Hrmph… That doesn't really give me an answer, though. I wanna know why they're chasing you… But I guess the details are a bit much for a little kid. I'll just have to ask one of them.*

"Sue, could you take her back to the dojo?"

"Umm… Sure! I'll explain what's happening to Yae and the others." I sent Sue and Iroha through a **[Gate]**. I knew they'd be safer with Yae and her family.

"My lord, they're here… Shall we?"

"Yeah, let's hear it from them." I turned around to face the six ninja who had just appeared in the back street. *Wait… There are more of you now? Geez…*

"Hey there! Did a girl go by here?!"

"I'm taking care of Iroha now. So why don't you tell m-"

The men immediately surrounded me and drew their weapons. I didn't even get a chance to ask them a question!

"[Shield]."

"Guh?!"

"Gah?!" Four of the men stopped after seeing two of their comrades blocked by an invisible wall. One of the ninjas struck my magical shield again before leaping back toward his allies.

"Bastard! You can use magic?!" There weren't many Eashenese people capable of casting spells, so seeing it in action was a rarity.

Instead, they had developed ninjutsu and special techniques. They were skills that had similar effects, but could only be gained through rigorous training.

I wondered if the ninja in front of me had such capabilities, but they probably did.

As I wondered that, the fattest of the men spewed fire from his mouth and sent it hurtling toward me. *What the... He can use ninjutsu?!* "Not so fast, wastrel!" Kohaku leaped in front of the incoming flames, emanating a shockwave that repelled them.

"Eek!! Uwaaah!" The tubby ninja, now caught on fire thanks to his own attack, started rolling around on the floor.

I shot out a little Water magic, since I didn't exactly want to kill him.

"Guh...!" The ninjas glared at me before throwing some small objects at the ground. *Oh, smoke bombs. I remember seeing this in old movies.*

I guess they're escaping under the smoke cover, then... Ah.

Before I noticed it, the ninjas were gone. I was honestly a little impressed. They'd gotten away.

"Not like you can keep away, though..." I casually pulled out my smartphone and ran a search for ninjas... The results shocked me. Several pins dropped on the map around Oedo. I wondered why the hell there were so many ninjas, were they holding a summit or something? But then again, the term ninja was pretty broad. It could've also been applying the terms to every shinobi in town.

I wondered if the Tokugawa ninjas were all at the castle or something... There were more than I'd expected.

Whatever, I just need to find out more info...

Then again, I should probably try to figure out whose ninjas these guys actually are... It could be a problem if they're serving the Tokugawa clan.

I sighed quietly and decided to head back to Yae's place. There were no enemies there, thankfully.

I opened up a **[Gate]** and made my way back. I walked into the dining room and found a tasty display of yellowtail sushi and radish on the table. *You're eating again…?!*

Sue looked up from the plate and spoke to me.

"Ah, Touya! Did you sort out the people who were chasing her?"

"Not exactly, no…" I explained what had happened, and Sue opened her eyes wide in surprise. Lu then walked in with a fresh serving of sushi. I couldn't believe they were still eating at a time like this. "Hey, Iroha. Just who are you?"

"I'm Iroha!"

That certainly wasn't much of an answer. As I was thinking of what to do with her, I heard a commotion come from the entrance. I wondered what it was.

"T-Touya-do… G-Grand Duke! Yae! Grand Duke…! A-Are you there?!"

The voice belonged to Jutaro. He was supposed to be at the castle. He sounded frantic, so I rushed toward the entryway to find him drenched in sweat. He was panting heavily and on the ground. He'd ran here full-pelt, and looked completely out of breath.

"Oh…Th-Thank goodness! T-Terrible things have happened… J-Just terrible!"

"Hold your horses, and calm down a moment. **[Refresh]**." I cast the restoration magic on him. I had no idea what was going on with him, but he needed to calm it. "T-Today there was a meeting of feudal lords at Oedo Castle… But the daughter of one of the lords has gone missing! There's a lot going on now and I'm not sure what to do, but from what I understand the Tokugawa security detail could be in great trouble for this! They almost rescued her, but she was captured in this very town!" *Hm?* "A-And I heard a report that the girl was almost found, but she was stolen away by a mysterious and powerful man who commanded a frightening beast!" *Uh oh.* I looked down at my feet for a moment. *Frightening beast... Mysterious and powerful...?*

"He could be an agent for political manipulation! How am I supposed to find him?! If I cannot find this fiend and kill him with my own hands, then Lord Tokugawa-sama's honor will be stained!"

"Uhm... About that... Whose daughter was she, exactly...?"

"Ah, f-forgive my impertinence! She is the young daughter of Lord Massamune-sama! And then, hm...? Grand Duke...?" I listened to Jutaro's words, but he quickly noticed that I was progressively sweating harder, and looking more flustered by the second.

This is definitely my bad.

Am I gonna get punished for this? Holy crap. Date Massamune? That one? The guy I met a while back? He seemed pretty nice, but definitely incapable of hiding his feelings.

But wait, isn't he only around my age?! How does he have a daughter at that age already? I know people marry young in this world but c'mon! Ack... Still, I need to focus here. This could cause a national incident... Better handle it fast.

I motioned for Jutaro to follow me and we walked into the living room.

The girl was eating some pickled radish as she turned to us. Even though she was wearing something so tattered, it seemed like Jutaro immediately recognized her noble status.

"G-Grand Duke... This girl..."

"Y-Yeah. My bad."

"Hm?"

"I-I will let them know at once!" Jutaro went charging out the entrance just as Yae and the others came walking inside.

"Oh, brother? I do wish he would stay a little longer, I do…"

"He'll be right back, I'm sure." I had a feeling he'd charge right there and then charge straight back. But it wasn't like I'd be there to cast [Refresh] on him at the castle.

Yae looked over to Sue and Iroha as they ate some more sushi together.

"Sue-dono… Who is this child?"

"That's Iroha."

"It seems like this kid is actually one of the feudal lords' daughters."

"I-Is that so, is it?! Could she be the child of Date Massamune, could she?!" Yae opened her eyes wide upon realizing who she was with. Sue just kind of shrugged and continued eating. Hilde and Lu didn't really seem all that fussed, either… But I guess those three were royalty anyway.

"Iroha, you're in Oedo because of your dad, right? Why'd you leave the castle?"

"Was bored… Daddy can't play with me. He promised he'd play when the meeting was over!! But it was so long…! That's why I went out to play."

"Didn't you think your father would get worried?"

"Don't know." She pouted quietly before explaining that she'd asked to go to the bathroom then snuck out of the small window in there. Apparently, she'd sneak out of the castle she lived in at home and play around often, so this kind of thing wasn't abnormal for her.

Apparently, Iroha could use magic, specifically Earth magic, which was rare for an Eashenese person. It was trivial for her to get out by manipulating the ground to make an escape route, or just tunneling through a wall.

"Your father still loves you, Iroha," said Sue.

"…Daddy hates me."

"No way. I love my father, and he loves me. Sometimes he can't be with me because he has to work, but when we're together we have a lot of fun. Time spent being upset with him, or thinking he's upset with you, is just wasted time."

"Mm…" Sue's father, Duke Ortlinde, was pretty busy a lot of the time. He had to deal with a lot of noble affairs, as well as diplomatic negotiations for his brother.

That's why he cherished the family time he could get. I definitely wanted to make sure he and Sue spent as much time together as they could before she came to live with me as my wife.

The little girl fell silent after listening to Sue's words.

I heard a sliding door being opened and the sound of running in the outside corridor.

"Iroha?!" The man that yelled out was none other than Date Massamune, the very same man that I'd met some time ago. He was wearing a beautiful dotted kimono. *Wait a second, guy. Your shoes are dirty!*

"Oh, Iroha! Are you okay?! Did he do anything to you?! You there! I cannot ever forgive you for this!" The feudal lord before me was glaring at me with a burning hatred in his eyes. It seemed he hadn't been fully briefed.

That reminded me, the last time I met him I was the masked warrior, Shirogane. This new first impression I'd made on him was definitely bad by comparison. Jutaro suddenly came running in from behind Lord Massamune. He'd come back faster than I expected, which made me think he must've met Massamune on the way to the castle. "D-Date-dono! P-Please do not speak in such a way to the grand duke! This is a m-misunderstanding, it is! I do hope you can compose yourself, I beg of you!"

"Enough of your prattling! Tokugawa's guard or not, you will pay for- Guauugh!" Date suddenly crumpled to the ground. He'd been struck in the head by someone who appeared from behind him. The man standing above the fallen lord was none other than Katakura Kohjuro Kagetsunna, Date's loyal retainer.

He'd struck his master in the side of the head with a sword sheath. I wondered if it was okay for retainers to do that. "Wh-Why did you do that, Kohjuro?!"

"Lord Massamune, please think of the current situation. Were you attempting to pick a fight with the leader of another nation? Please use your head." Seemed like this guy had some sense. I was glad to hear it. I didn't mind exactly, but I had to consider Ieyahsu as well. Since I was here under his care, I didn't want to trigger tensions between him and Massamune.

Iroha suddenly stood up and walked toward her father.

"Daddy... Sue and Touya were really nice to me... They aren't bad."

"I-Is that right?"

"You always get like this, Daddy. Mommy's gonna get mad at you if she finds out."

"Gah!" It was smart of her to involve her mother in this. I could already sense who wore the pants in that marriage. It reminded me of the Xenoahs overlord.

Iroha continued to talk in front of her fussing father.

"I did a bad thing. I'm sorry I ran away from the castle. I just wanted to play and I was really bored..."

"Iroha..." Massamune clambered up until he was on his knees, then leaned forward to embrace his daughter. She hugged him back, placing her little hand on the small of his neck. Everyone in the room let out a small sigh of relief.

"I'm sorry. It was my idea to bring you to Oedo to begin with, but I got distracted with work and ended up taking much too long. Please forgive me for that, Iroha."

"It's OK! I saw a lot of Oedo... And I had some tasty dumplings and some yummy fish. It was really fun."

"I am happy to hear that..." Iroha began to giggle. Massamune smiled earnestly back. He didn't look even a shadow of the upset man he was a few moments ago.

I still felt it was a shame they didn't get to see the sights together, though. I suddenly got an idea, then turned to Kohjuro.

"Will you be heading back home from Oedo after the meetings are over?"

"That should be right... It would take around nine or ten days to return home. We cannot move too quickly due to Iroha-sama." My question was answered fairly promptly.

Unlike other nations, Eashen wasn't as developed. They didn't have standardized transportation like carriages. They had a lot of rocky roads, so traveling that far would be pretty rough even on horseback. I wasn't sure if I'd be able to stomach it.

That's why I decided to make a proposal.

"I'll send you all back to your home in ten or so days using my [Gate] spell, alright? Don't worry about fees or anything, I'll just let you all through."

"Hm... I would truly appreciate that, but why would you do such a thing for us?"

"Because we're friends, you dummy! This is nothing, no big deal at all!" Sue said as she suddenly stomped over and planted her hands on her hips, staring Massamune down.

"Thank you, Sue!" Iroha smiled and hugged Sue. I was glad that things would likely go smoothly from here and was even more glad to see that Iroha and her father were happy.

"I wonder what on earth just happened, I do... Sue-dono is powerful..."

"Sue certainly has the ability to make fast friends."

"Yae, Hilde, would you like to try some of my sushi?" Yae, Hilde, and Lu were all looking over the scene from the dining table.

With that, all matters were settled. Ieyahsu came to the house not long after and returned to his castle with Iroha, Massamune, and an entourage of black-clad ninja.

Eashen wasn't a member of the League of Nations, so I couldn't give him a smartphone, but I gifted Massamune a Gate Mirror so Iroha could exchange letters with Sue. I was happy she'd made such a nice friend.

I thanked Ieyahsu for the rice he'd given me and informed him that I'd be taking the Date party home ten days from then.

It seemed like the meeting between the feudal lords wasn't quite over yet. The fallout from the monkey incident was still in full swing, and they were still unsure as to what to do with the territory that once belonged to the Hashiba house.

Apparently, the emperor himself was coming as well, to bestow honors or something like that. I think he was going to name the newest feudal lord or something... But I didn't want to get too involved in that.

They'd be done with it all in about two days, so that gave Massamune and his daughter plenty of time to sightsee.

I'd never met the emperor of Eashen, though... It would certainly be interesting to see him.

If I met the emperor, I could ask him if he wanted to join the League of Nations. I wondered if it'd be okay though, Eashen wasn't exactly a whole nation or anything...

As I thought about those issues, I said goodbye to Yae's family and headed home with the others.

"...So that's what happened."

"Yeah, it was rough. But I'm glad I managed to reconcile them both."

"I agree." Leen brought the mochi up to her mouth. The girls were gathered around the table, eating mochi and different snacks.

"Which do you like the most?"

"Uhhm… I like them both, but I think the taste of this one is a little more refined… Don't you think?"

"Guh… I guess even though I was taught the recipe, I'm still not quite good enough." Lu looked over the sushi that Linze and Sakura had tried. It seemed they preferred the taste of Yae's mother's.

Hmm, I dunno. I couldn't really tell the difference. I think if you keep trying to chase perfection like that, Lu, you might not succeed.

"This mochi thing is amazing! Can't you make this, Lu?" Elze grinned at Lu, attempting to distract her from her grumbling. Then she reached down and took another bite of mochi.

"Um… I don't know the details of the recipe exactly, but it doesn't look too hard to reproduce. I'm sure I could make it. I think it's made with rice? I'm not sure, though… I could learn a little more from Aer."

"It is not ordinary rice, it is not. And it cannot be too watery, it cannot! You should be able to use the rice we received from Ieyahsu-sama." That reminded me, he'd given us a small amount of rice bran for dessert use.

I was glad Yae reminded me, because I'd put it in [**Storage**] and totally forgot. Still, food wouldn't spoil in there so it was fine.

"Do you just cook it like ordinary rice, then?"

"Uhh… Not exactly. Here, gimme a sec."

I used my smartphone to look up how to pound mochi and sent it to Lu's phone. She checked the page immediately.

"Touya-dono. We should pound mochi together next time, we should. I would like everyone to be able to partake."

"Yeah, that'd be fun. Everyone should enjoy it." The population of Brunhild was mostly Eashenese. A large chunk of our knights were Eashenese, too. It'd be fun to get a whole group exercise together. I'm sure they'd find it nostalgic.

I showed the others the video of mochi pounding, and they all seemed interested. I definitely wasn't as fast as the guys in the video, though.

I turned to the girls and asked them if there were any foods in particular that they'd like to be made.

Kinako mochi… natto… Isobemaki, ankoro mochi, and zoni… They ended up wanting a lot of stuff, including a few dishes that had more of a New Years kind of feel to them. Dumplings were just better to eat in general, though… So that was my preference.

Sue looked at the video as it continued to play and then looked at me.

"Touya… Can we invite Iroha to Brunhild next time? I wanna play with her some more."

"Sure. We'll be sure to prepare a bunch of Eashenese stuff to welcome her." I decided when that time came, I'd invite Yae's family and Ieyahsu to join us as well. I wanted them to have fun in Brunhild.

Lu continued to feverishly attempt to exceed the quality of Nanae's dish, but eventually, even she had to admit that the Eashenese housewife was simply far beyond her skill level.

"Welcome back, Master Touya. Welcome back, madams."

"Ping!"

"Pong!"

"Pang!"

Shirogane bowed lightly, and the three Gollems by his side followed suit. Seemed like they were learning well.

We'd come back to the Reverse World to see if the massive Phrase invasion in Sandora ended up having any effect on this side.

The regular Phrase were seeking the Sovereign Core, so there'd be no reason for them to come to the Reverse World, but the metal devils were different. I was concerned that a large number of those types might've come out into this world, so I decided to investigate.

I did a search on my map for them, but no hits came up. Thankfully it seemed like my fears were for naught.

"Hey, Touya! Do you think he was including me when he said madams just now, huh? Huh?!"

"Absolutely not. He just meant to say madams and you."

"You mean madams and mistress, right?" I rolled my eyes as Doctor Babylon grinned at me.

I'd brought five people with me this time. Babylon, Yumina, Lu, Linze, and Leen.

Sue, Elze, Yae, Sakura, and Hilde had things to take care of so they passed. Sue was with family, Elze, Yae, and Hilde were training with the knight order, and Sakura was helping her mother at the school.

I only came to check if any of the Mutated Constructs had come in, so frankly I didn't have anything else to do in the Reverse World. But Leen and Linze said they wanted to read for a while in the library, and Doc Babylon said she wanted to check out a city since she didn't get to leave the house last time.

I figured that it'd be a waste to just pop in and go straight back, so I decided to take her around. Yumina and Lu decided they'd tag along, too.

"Alright, let's go to the Theocracy's capital, then."

"We can eat while we're there, too."

"Sounds good…" I opened up a [Gate] to the capital and brought us to a back alley near the main street.

We walked out to see the regular hustle and bustle.

I picked up a newspaper and we all headed toward the cafe we dined at the last time.

It was already mid-afternoon, so there were a few vacant spots. I ordered a few snacks, as well as a drink from their menu called "kophee." Judging from the scent… It was just coffee.

As I picked at my food, I scanned the newspaper in front of me. If Leen were with us, she'd have absolutely told me off for having poor table manners.

"Newspapers are definitely useful, huh… Maybe we can introduce a printing press to Brunhild."

"The world doesn't have much in the way of long-distance communication technology right now. We could mass produce stuff using Babylon, but we don't want it to open up the floodgates for stuff like propaganda or fake news. It'd be handy, but we don't need to make all the social developments. Let's just wait and see if they manage it themselves." I shrugged my shoulders and took a sip of my kophee before passing the paper to the Doctor. *Yep, that's coffee. It's a little bitter, though... Needs sugar.*

"Oho?" Doctor Babylon made a weird noise as her eyes fixed on a certain part of the paper. Her eyes narrowed as she dug around in her pocket, produced a small lens, and looked through it to inspect the news. *You just carry around a magnifying glass?* "What is it?"

"Well... Look at this article." I read the headline she was pointing at. It said, "Pirate Ship Drifts Ashore At Barköl Harbor."

"Huh...? Let's see... Unidentified ship, assumed to be pirate, drifted in at Barköl harbor... The entire crew of thirty-four men has been apprehended... What about it?"

"Look at the photo of the wrecked ship. Right here. Look at the emblem on the sails. It's tattered, but don't you get it yet?" *Hm? Emblem?* I borrowed Doc Babylon's magnifying glass and looked closer at the black-and-white image. It was certainly a wreck of a ship, alright.

I looked carefully and realized what I was looking at. An emblem of a unicorn, a shield, and stars. I was completely floored. "That's the Rcfrcesc National Emblem!" I stared down at the image in absolute shock. It couldn't be... And yet it was. The ship that had gone missing a while back. The McClane. I skimmed my eyes over the rest of the article and found that the ship had crashed into the harbor and washed ashore, and the crewmen had all been apprehended under the orders of the man who ruled Barköl. They couldn't speak the language of this world, so they had no way of defending themselves.

"But why would a Refreese ship be in this world?"

"I have no idea... God said that people could drift between worlds now and then, but this is ridiculous..." I shrugged my shoulders as I answered Lu, but my mind was abuzz. *Is this just a coincidence? Or is this related to the weird stuff lately?*

"Well, we can't just leave them alone. Let's go help them out."

"Hold on a second. What do you plan on doing afterward, hm? Return them home?"

"Well, obviously, I... Oh... Oh."

"Use your head. If you rescue them like that, you'll have to explain the Reverse World to them. Not just the crewmen, but also the Refreese government, and then the other world leaders too! I don't think the world is ready for that yet." She had a point. I couldn't expect the other world leaders to accept this matter as nonchalantly as my fiancees did. Well, there was a chance they'd understand due to the Phrase, but it was still a bad idea.

"There should be a spell from the Dark school that hypnotizes people, right?"

"You mean [**Hypnosis**], right? We could definitely use that to alter their memories, yeah."

There were a lot of ancient Dark spells that could manipulate people mentally. I could use those spells to manipulate memories, confuse people, send them into frenzies, consume them with lust, make them lose their sanity, or even just turn them downright braindead. Frankly, those spells scared me.

I didn't really want to use spells like that against anyone who wasn't a really horrific villain, but I had no real choice in this situation. Plus, they'd been thrown into jail in a foreign land with no knowledge of what their captors were even saying, they'd probably be happy to lose memories like that.

I'd read up on [**Hypnosis**] in the Babylon Library before, so I was sure I knew how to use it.

"Alright, let's go save them. Seems like that harbor is in the Panaches Kingdom." I used my map to check where the place was, taking care not to project the hologram since we were in a public space.

"It seems to cover the territories of Palouf and Lihnea in our world... Palnea island." Yumina muttered to herself as she looked over the map. She wasn't wrong, it was basically identical, just flipped.

It was quite a bit away from Allent, though.

"I'll fly over there, okay? You guys sit tight while I do that."

"Alright. Please take care."

I could've used [Teleport], but I was still a bit scarred from the last time. I decided not to be lazy, since it'd only take about thirty minutes.

I headed into a back alley and cast [Invisible], then shot off into the sky with [Fly]. I applied [Accel] for good measure and rocketed away like a missile.

After a while, I had a good view of the sea below me. Soon enough I saw the coastline of Palnea island, or rather, the Panaches Kingdom.

I landed in the harbor, which was found in the south-east, and immediately opened up a [Gate] to the back alley near the cafe I'd left behind. Then I got the girls and headed back through the portal.

"There are a lot of ships here... Some of them look strange." Lu looked around the harbor with curious eyes.

There were plenty of docked ships without any sails. *Are they steam-powered? Or maybe magic?* I looked over to the pier and saw several men and Gollems hauling cargo. *Wait...That ship has arms. Is it a Gollem itself?* I walked along the harbor and saw several fresh fish for sale. The pungent smell of raw fish hit me right in the nose, but it wasn't too bad. Seemed like they were keeping the fish cool with ice generated by Gollems.

As I continued walking, we reached a place filled with the tasty scent of grilled fish. *Steel yourself, Touya... No getting distracted... Oh... Is that steamed sea snail...?*

"Touya, look!" Yumina pointed toward a crashed ship on the shoreline. I could see the tattered sail hanging from the snapped mast. It bore Refreese's emblem, there was no doubt about it.

We got close enough to see the nameplate engraved on the side of the ship. Sure enough, it said McClane.

"Well, guess there's no denying it now." The ship managed to just barely survive, much like the man it shared a name with.

I hailed a nearby sailor and asked him about how the ship came to be claimed by the local authorities.

He said that about four days prior, the ship made landfall after a harsh storm. There were thirty-four survivors aboard, and the rest were apparently dead.

The officials in the area tried to ask them questions about how they got there, but neither party could speak with one another, so the inquest went nowhere.

They tried to hand over a map so the crew could point out where they were from, but for some reason, the men tried to flip the map upside down, and they just got stressed about it. The crews were also scared by the sight of the Gollems. Some of the crew buckled under their own stress and started to raise a fuss, so ultimately all the men were subdued and put into prison.

They found weapons and cannons aboard the ship, so it was suggested that they were part of a pirate band that had been causing trouble in the area. *Welp... They're part of the navy, so the weapons make sense...*

"Kind of ironic that they originally set off to take out the pirates, only to be branded as pirates..." I felt a little sad for them, in all honesty.

Their fate hadn't yet been decided, but if they were found guilty of piracy they'd surely be executed. I needed to hurry up and get them out.

The prison they'd been put in was a small building next to the harbor security dorm.

It was still midday, but that didn't mean much to my magic. We headed toward the building. It was made of something that looked like concrete and had a fairly dull design to it.

There was only a single guard at the entrance, probably because it was the afternoon.

There were all kinds of people walking up and down the street, and any commotion would attract attention from nearby. That was probably the reason for such short staff. Either way, we were lucky for it.

"[Invisible]."

We walked to a quiet area nearby, and I made everyone invisible. We walked right past the guard and made our way into the entryway. There was a staircase ahead that led to a jail area.

There were three cells in total, with roughly ten men in each. The men looked powerless and miserable like the fight was completely gone from them. Some were even sobbing.

I used [Silence] in a small radius to prevent the guard upstairs from hearing us. That would prevent even a large commotion from being noticed.

I then undid my spell. The crewmen, who saw the appearance of sudden invaders, instinctively cowered away from us.

"Is your captain here?"

"Y-You can speak our language?!"

"I can. I also know you guys were hunting pirates outside of Refreese." The men looked shocked as a scruffy, red-bearded man pushed his way forward and spoke to us.

"You can call me Simmons. I'm second-in-command. We lost our captain when he fell overboard."

"What happened to you exactly? Please tell me all you can." Simmons looked down with a mournful face as he began to recount what happened.

"I... I don't know... On that day we were headed to the pirate hideouts with the others. But all of a sudden, this weird mist set in around us at all sides. It was strange... Way too strange. The weather was fine until it suddenly changed... The mist got deeper and deeper... And swirled around us, and I swear it started glowing a dark gold. The golden mist swallowed us all up, and we lost all sense of direction... Our compass just broke, it didn't work at all. We couldn't navigate by the sun or stars, either. Then when the mist vanished, we got caught in a storm. We held on for dear life, and some of us didn't make it... When the storm ended, we washed ashore right here. We celebrated, cause we thought we were saved... But we weren't. These strangers didn't understand us, and we didn't understand them. They didn't even know the country we were from. They have all these weird ships, and these strange iron animals I've never seen before. Hey, tell me! Where are we? What are those iron animals? Why was the map backwa—"

"Tempt, o Dark! Implanted Falsehood: [Hypnosis]." I'd heard enough and triggered my spell before Simmons finished.

A purple mist began to spread through the air, clouding the eyes of all the men in the jail.

"Listen to me. You were separated from the Refreese fleet and attacked by sea monsters. You got out of it, but your ship was wrecked in a storm and washed up on an uncharted island. The stress of your starvation and extreme conditions caused you to see weird hallucinations. That's what those weird ships and iron animals were. They were just wild visions. Just dreams."

"...Just... Dreams..." The crewmen just stared back with vacant eyes. I hoped that'd be enough.

Lu asked me if that was morally justifiable treatment, but I thought it was probably better for their long-term mental health to convince them that their trauma wasn't real. Plus they had met with a storm, so the story was still kinda true.

In the end, their trip to the Reverse World would just be a bad dream.

I opened up the cells and then opened up a portal to Drakliff island. Yumina and the others guided the men through.

They walked slowly and unsteadily, like zombies.

Once the girls were through the [Gate], I left the prison through the same way I'd entered. I walked up to the McClane's wreck and stashed it in my [Storage], then immediately left for Drakliff island before anyone noticed.

I was sure that a vanishing shipwreck would definitely attract prying eyes before long.

I wanted to get those men back to the regular world as soon as possible. It wouldn't be good for them to remain in that state for long.

All of a sudden, my smartphone started to vibrate. It was an incoming call... And the one calling was none other than God Almighty.

"Uhh... 'Sup?"

"Ah, hello there, Touya. Seems like you found a little bit of trouble, hm?"

"Yeah, I'll say... Were you watching?"

"Indeed. There was something I wanted to tell you, you see. It is related to the issue you have been facing recently... Would you mind paying me a little visit?" I wondered what God Almighty wanted from me so bad that I had to go up there and see him. I said I'd visit him when I had a chance, then ended the call.

Hmm... Did a problem happen in the other world or something? I wonder what the issue is...

Oh, crap. Can't spend too much time thinking about it. I got people to relocate.

I sighed quietly as I walked to the Dimensional Disruptor Mk. II and fired it up.

◇　◇　◇

We brought the McClane crew back to the regular world, and dumped off the shipwreck on a shoreline not far from Refreese, along with the men themselves.

They woke up a small amount of time later and saw the coastline over the stretch of water. They immediately started swimming toward land and made it without any trouble. There was a small road nearby that led toward a fishing town, so I felt they'd be safe from there.

They'd stick to the script I gave them via the [Hypnosis] spell, so I was sure it'd be fine.

"Guess we can take it easy now."

"I'm glad they're safe." We kept an eye on the men from the shadows to ensure they got to the village safely. The villagers clothed and fed them, then the men recounted their story. It seemed like the whole story with the Reverse World had been rendered as a mere hazy dream.

I opened up a [Gate] and we all headed back to Brunhild.

I still had no idea how the McClane sailed to the other side, though…

There were examples of people being spirited away in this world, much like my own… But I wondered if them going to the Reverse World was really just a random coincidence.

On the subject of being spirited away, I remembered that I needed to spirit myself away to meet God Almighty. I figured I could probably ask him more about what happened.

I told Yumina and the others that I was heading out for a while, then headed to the kitchen to pick up some pudding, cake, dorayaki, and other treats as a gift for the old man. Crea wasn't in, so I was basically sneaking treats from the kitchen without permission... I made a mental note to apologize if she was mad about it later.

"Alright, I'm off."

"Give him my regards, you know?" Karen was in the kitchen eating some cake, so I told her where I was going. I had a feeling I'd be blamed for the cake she'd taken, too...

I fired up a [Gate] to the Divine Realm, and immediately stepped out to see God Almighty in his regular room, seated on his cushion.

"Good day, Touya."

"Hey, it's been a while. Here, I brought you some snacks."

"Oh, thank you so much." God Almighty took the little box of desserts and put the pudding and cake into his mini-fridge, and then placed the plate of dorayaki in the middle of the table alongside some fresh tea.

"So what was it you wanted to tell me?"

"Well... I do wonder where I should start... I think I should explain to you how I... Or rather, how we gods are placed as patrons of worlds." God Almighty started to mutter a bit as he stroked his beard.

"As I am sure you know, the number of worlds that we gods survey is immeasurable. But what we manage when we oversee these worlds are not necessarily the worlds on a micro level. We, for example, cannot interfere with civilizations that may develop there, even if the civilization was headed on a path of death and destruction. In the end, death and destruction is just as natural as life, after all. The worlds that head toward such a fate are typically dealt with by the god of destruction; that is his job, you see. It works in tandem with mine. I typically birth new worlds once he eliminates one." *Huh… This god of destruction guy sounds pretty casual, contrary to his scary name…*

"Now, it is not just ruined worlds that the god of destruction watches… There are also deviant worlds. For example, a world in which a wicked god has managed to gestate, and all preventative measures have fallen through…"

"W-Wait a second… You can't mean…"

"Fret not. The world you live in right now is not yet classed as a deviant world. The wicked god has yet to descend and cause chaos there. But… I am afraid to say that it is on the cusp of such a status." *Wait… Does he mean that if the wicked god starts mobilizing, then the whole world could get annihilated by the gods?* "And that is not the sole problem… The wicked god birthed from events in your world has been spawning familiars and causing trouble in the space between worlds. Look here, if you could." God Almighty raised his right hand toward the small table, and suddenly a 3D hologram of the world I lived in was projected atop it.

He then raised his left hand, and a 3D map of the Reverse World appeared next to it. The two worlds were symmetrically lined up as if there was a mirror between the two maps. I also couldn't believe it had taken me this time to realize it, but both of the worlds appeared to be completely flat.

"This was the state of the two worlds in relation to each other about half a year ago. However…"

The two worlds gradually began to grow closer and closer, until there was a slight overlap on the two maps.

"This is how the two worlds look in relation to each other right now. The wicked god and its spawn are attempting to fuse these worlds. Or rather... They may have already succeeded to an extent."

"What?!" I knew that the Mutated Constructs and the McClane appearing in the Reverse World had to mean something... But I had no idea something as insane as this was even possible. "Why would the wicked god do that?"

"By merging the two worlds together, they would become a single world. Or rather, a new world entirely, one that was not born from me. That would separate it from my influence entirely. I am sure the servile god who died to the beast originally planned something like this, and they are merely continuing it."

"That's crazy!" I had no idea what the implications of that even were. "Now... These deviant worlds are typically dealt with by the god of destruction after a collective divine consensus. If we were to leave it be, it would be possible for it to generate negative effects and start influencing other worlds, after all. That certainly would not be something we want." God Almighty's eyes pierced right through me, causing me to instinctively gulp in fear.

"And that is why... We have reached a consensus. We will have you handle this situation, Touya."

"Excuse me?!"

Hold up! How's that the consensus you came to?!

"Please handle the disturbance between these two worlds as best you can. If you can achieve this, then by my authority as the god of worlds, I will formally recognize you as a fully-fledged God. A High God."

"Whaaaat?!" *But that's higher ranked than Karen, Moroha, and the others! Can you even do that?!* "In all honesty… I expect these two worlds to remain connected. We do not have a god in place to be patron of this new joined world. It will certainly become a new world, one that would cause me no end of hassle to reclassify. That is why I wish for you to become its patron in my stead, Touya."

"What? There's just no way I can do that! I'd be a fake god at best!"

"You are no fake, my boy… No pale imitation. It is not a difficult task, either. All you need to do is ensure that the god of destruction has no reason to move in on your world. It will be your territory."

Isn't that exactly what's happening right now while it's your territory?! Is this really okay?!

"It is not as if you would ascend to such a status immediately, anyway. You will be more than permitted to spend time down there in order to continue your training period."

"For how long, exactly?"

"Let me see… Roughly two or three-thousand years should do."

That's extremely goddamn long, what the hell! I'm pretty sure the God Co. Ltd would be guilty of an overly long training term for new employees if it was a real company! So… Hold on, let me get this straight. I'm the new hire at this place… And I'm spending two or three thousand years in training, and then on the first day of my job, I'll be promoted to management?! This is a messed up command structure, old man!

"Did you already decide this?"

"Not at all. It is quite fine if you say no, of course. You can take the path of working up the ladder from the lowest ranks. But that would leave your world in my hands, and I am quite sure it would become a deviant world before long… If it was determined as potentially harmful to other worlds, then we would have no choice but to annihilate it. It would be quite the waste if you went to all the trouble of dealing with the wicked god only for that to happen."

"...I don't really have an option here, do I..."

"You will have to forgive me. I had planned on a method that wouldn't cause as much of a fuss, but it is still rather messy..."

"No, I get it. Even if I didn't do anything, the god of destruction would destroy the world and the wicked god alike, right? I'm just glad I might have a chance to fix this mess... Plus I kind of want to give that thing what's coming to it, since it's been causing trouble for everyone." I shrugged and chugged my now-lukewarm tea. This was indeed troubling, but I knew it was inevitable. I didn't exactly think I was management material, but I had a feeling two or three thousand years of training might help.

All I had to do was beat the snot outta that wicked god.

"I am glad you accepted these terms, Touya. I would be rather sad if that world came to ruin, too." God Almighty sighed and slowly drank his tea. I wondered if he'd developed a little bit of a soft spot for the people of that world after spending some time there.

"So if that world was judged worthy of destruction... What would happen to me and the others?"

"You and your dependents, those girls closest to you, would be picked up and evacuated to a safer world. Then everything would be obliterated by the god of destruction, reduced to mere dust."

His response was honestly harrowing. Everyone in my country, all the world leaders, everyone I knew... They'd be gone forever. I didn't even want to consider such an option.

Whether it was the Phrase or the wicked god, the god of destruction would've been tasked with taking care of it eventually. The only thing that made a difference was the fact that I lived in that world. That's why I had to do my best.

I steeled myself and firmly resolved to work as hard as I could.

And that immediately went right out the window when I got home. I found myself frantically rolling left and right on my bed in a panic. The responsibility was way too much after actually thinking about it.

"Me? Managing a world? What the hell? How can I do that when I suck at managing this country?" I continued to thrash and grumble as I squeezed a pillow to my chest. *Guh... I'm worrying way too much... I need to take care of that wicked god... Auuugh...*

"But... Guh... Gaaah!!" I felt like the receptionist at a business suddenly being given a task way out of his depth. *Why would you trust the receptionist with something like that?!*

Urgh... Usually, I could just ask a trusted higher-up to help me, but...

"No way that'd work... The only person out of that lot who's even vaguely reliable is uncle Kousuke..." *Ugh... A love life gossip, a battle junkie, a hunting enthusiast, a music maniac, and a tiny drunk are my only alternatives... Kousuke's not exactly good at anything except agriculture, either...*

It was true that they were lower-tier, specialized gods... It wasn't exactly their fault they only had one focus, but still...

"Are you okay?"

"Yeah... Just grumbling about some annoying stuff..." I heard a voice, prompting me to sit upright on the bed. It was Yumina, wearing her pajamas. She looked really cute in them.

"What brings you here...?"

"You seemed stressed earlier... You didn't eat much at dinnertime and seemed distracted. I wanted to see if you were okay."

"Oh...Sorry for worrying you." *Geez, I really am useless. How can someone like me manage a whole world if I can't even keep my fiancee from being worried? Ugh... I gotta stop dwelling on this, this sucks.*

"So? Did something happen? Can't you tell me?"

"Well… It's just…" I'd already told Yumina and the others about my divinity, and I figured that since they were my dependents on a divine level, they had a right to know about what was troubling me.

I told Yumina exactly what happened between me and God Almighty up there. I tried to word it delicately, hoping she wouldn't be too scared about the idea of the world being destroyed.

"I see… So that's what you're upset about?"

"Mhm… I have to do the work of a real god all of a sudden… I mean… It'll still be a while before I actually have to do it, but knowing it's there is kinda scary." I laughed bitterly. I honestly felt a little pitiful showing this side of me, but it wasn't like I could hide it.

"It's going to be okay. You can do this, Touya."

"I appreciate your support, but I'm still uneasy…"

"It'll be okay. I know it will be. This world and the other one are going to be fine. It's you, Touya. I know you'll pull through." I looked up, finding her mismatched eyes staring right back at me. I really wondered where that level of confidence came from… Honestly, though… I was happy she thought so highly of me.

"Plus you're not alone, silly. So don't carry this burden on your shoulders alone. We'll all work with each other, okay? We'll make it through. I promise. There are all kinds of people who'd be willing to help you!"

Yumina let out an innocent smile and closed her eyes. Her kindness pierced right through me, prompting an instinctive response to lunge forward and pull her close in a big hug.

"I'm sorry for worrying you. You're right… I have all of you. We'll face any challenge together… I'm sorry I have to ask this of you, but I'll be counting on you, okay?"

"Mhm…" Yumina hugged me back just as tightly. I was so thankful that I'd met her, and all the others.

They were irreplaceable. Not just them, everyone I'd met so far on this crazy journey in another world… They were precious and kind. I had to protect the world for the sake of the people living in it. Real feelings of courage began to well up within me.

"No fair… How come Yumina gets to do that…?"

"Shh, Sue! Don't blow our cover!" *Wait, what was that?!* I suddenly looked across the room. I then realized the abnormalities in the space around me.

There were a few distended curtains, an open closet with misplaced clothes, my chair wasn't pushed in all the way under my desk, and I could see a foot poking out from behind my bookcase.

"How long have you guys been there?!"

"Since you were rolling around on the bed…"

"That's since the beginning!" Elze and the others came out from their hiding spots with guilty faces. Even Paula was there.

Was I really so out of it that I didn't notice they were hiding in my room while I was having my meltdown?! "Why were you guys hiding to begin with?"

"Well… We ended up having a talk about who would come to comfort you…"

"Yumina-dono is very talented at rock-paper-scissors, she is." Seemed like they were doing silly things again. I was about to sigh when Sue came bounding toward me.

"Listen up, Touya! It's not just about you! We're here too, you big dummy! We're the strongest family in the world, right? No way we could lose to that Destruction guy!"

…The god of destruction isn't our enemy, Sue… I sighed and smiled. The fact they felt that way made me happy. Sue then jumped up and hugged me like Yumina did, and then grinned mischievously. Just as I wondered what she was up to, she kissed me on the cheek.

"H-Hey! Don't you dare try to get one up on us, little missy!"

"Th-That's right! Just because you're the youngest doesn't mean you can get one over us!"

"...I won't lose..." Elze and Linze started walking toward me, but Sakura nimbly slipped between them and kissed me on the other cheek before they could even get close.

"Whaaaat?!" screamed all the girls in unison. That prompted a stampede, as all of them came charging toward me. *G-Girls, please! I'm flattered, but you can't all kiss me at the same time! Augh! W-Wait, is someone trying to undo my belt buckle?! What the... Paula?! What are you doing?! Quit that!* I ended up under a dogpile of fiancees, but I was happy. I knew that together, we could overcome anything.

◇　◇　◇

I was glad that I was resolved to do something, but that meant I had to put some action behind my words.

The elimination of the Phrase and the mutants would carry on as usual for the time being... But I wanted to see if I could mitigate the inevitable panic when the Reverse World and the actual world fused together.

Though... Expecting people not to panic when their entire world becomes twice as big and connected to another land with an entirely different culture would be a bit much.

I was sure there'd be mass confusion on both sides.

That's why I knew what I wanted to do next.

"You wanna learn how to traverse different worlds?" I brought up the subject during breakfast, while Karen was hungrily chowing down her toast, and Moroha was gulping down her morning tea.

"Why would you wanna... Oh, because of what we talked about earlier?"

"Yeah. Being able to use that ability would make it a lot easier to switch between the two worlds." I didn't want to have to go to Babylon every time I wanted to make a trip to the Reverse World. Frankly, I'd been shying away from learning that ability since I didn't want to lose any more of my humanity, but it seemed like becoming a god was inevitable at this point.

"Well... We'd be fine teaching you that, yeah. We're here to help you out and stuff, so don't worry."

"Umm... The only issue is that there isn't really anything to teach, you know?"

"What do you mean?" Karen, who had now finished her toast, said something that surprised me.

"Using the ability to travel across worlds is basically the same as regular transportation magic, you know? It'd be fine if you can grasp that, and you already can. All you gotta do is come with me through a few worlds to get a feel for it, and you should be set, you know?" *Through a few worlds...? Does she mean worlds other than this one and the Reverse world?* "So which one of you will show me?"

"I just said so, you know? Go around with me. Moroha is gonna be training with the knights today. I'm fine with it, you know? I think it'll take you about a day to get the fundamentals down." Karen drank her tea down then stood up. *Is that really something I can get down in a day? I'd rather be spared from anything too brutal or taxing...*

The two of us went out to the courtyard.

"Okay! Channel that divinity of yours through your whole body, you know? When you feel it envelop you, you gotta let it seep out through your pores, you know? Don't activate a full Apotheosis, just let it gently smother you all over the place." I did as she instructed and let my own divinity flow through me, spreading it out a little.

I was surprised by how well I could control it, even to such a fine degree. It seemed like I'd improved without realizing.

"Mm… That's good! So make sure you focus, you know? We'll try jumping worlds now." Karen reached out and grabbed my hand, and I suddenly felt a lurching sensation as my body felt as if it was moving upward.

I felt as if I was being pulled upward by a bungee cord, but the sensation was suddenly cut short by a pressing force of gravity. My body felt like it weighed six times as much… It was terrible!

"Guh…"

"Woo! We did it!"

Karen grinned, prompting me to look at my surroundings. We stood across a vast, rocky plain. There were rocks rolling around in the wind here and there, and the sky itself was a rusty red.

It was like the depiction of Mars from this one sci-fi movie I saw as a kid. I couldn't totally recall the title. There was nothing around but a dustbowl. I just saw red rocks and dry sands.

"…This is another world?"

"That's right. It's hard to explain, but this world is about as old and developed as the one we just came from, you know? It just has fewer people…" I asked her to explain further, and she told me that this world was fairly advanced, but a world war broke out. The resulting carnage turned the air and ground toxic, and the very planet became inhospitable to human life. The survivors were living in underground domes, apparently.

Karen then went on to explain that if we weren't using our divinity, then the toxins in the air would've rotted our lungs and caused us to shrivel up and die. It was quite harrowing, all in all.

"Well, it isn't too rare for apex predators to have that role stripped from them, you know? Look over there." Karen pointed over in a direction and I saw a tiny, six-legged frog-like creature scuttling around the rocks. It had adapted and was getting around just fine, it seemed.

"That species might end up taking this world over someday, you know?" She had a point. There was the Cretaceous—Paleogene extinction event sixty-six million years ago on Earth. There were a lot of proposed theories as to why that ended up happening. There was the theory that it was a meteorite, rising sea levels, natural decline of the species, volcanic eruptions, pathogens, a shifting of the poles, and some even believed aliens did it. It looked like that kind of thing happened everywhere.

I wondered if the Phrase counted as an extinction event in action.

"Alright! On to the next, you know?" My hyperactive older sister grabbed my hand again, and the bungee-jump sensation overtook my body once more. It was horrible...

When the feeling subsided, I opened my eyes to see a beautiful grassy plain spreading out before me. A gentle breeze carried a sweet scent in the air. Clouds drifted through the skies, and there were even a few peaceful looking mountains in the distance. It was a far cry from the last world I'd experienced.

"Guess it's an ordinary world this time..."

"The concept of the ordinary is fundamentally subjective, you know? This world doesn't have a single animal in it, actually."

"Wait, what?" When Karen said that, I did notice how quiet things were. There wasn't a single bird in the sky, nor did I see any insects or rodents scampering about in the grass. This world was a world of plants.

Wait, then how does pollination work? Don't they need bugs for that at least? What about the soil? Don't earthworms help enrich it and stuff...?

As I mused to myself, Karen bent down and pulled out a tuft of grass. Almost immediately, an identical tuft shot out of the ground and replaced it. *What...* I stared in disbelief and repeated her motion, pulling out a handful of grass myself. Just like before, the empty patch was immediately filled out. I had no idea how that worked.

It seemed like applying my standards of sense to a foreign world was pointless. It wasn't like it had to abide by the rules I knew.

"Alright, let's gooo!"

"Already?!" Karen didn't even bother explaining what was up with the grassy world. Instead, she grabbed my hand and we went shooting off.

After that, we passed through countless realities. I didn't even know how many we went through by the end of it, but it helped me grasp just how to move through dimensions.

It was kind of like **[Teleport],** I had to develop a strong visualization of what I was aiming for, and then seek out the world I wanted.

A metaphor used once was that the worlds were positioned kind of like steps on a staircase. If you know which step you're on, then you should be able to take steps up, down, or even diagonally.

Plus, any world I'd been to before would be easily revisited similarly to how I used **[Gate].**

"So, time to try it yourself, you know? Head back home! If you get lost, I'll find you." I closed my eyes and tried to visualize the position of my home in the vast universe. *Uhh... I think it's around... Here, maybe?*

I triggered the jump. I'd gotten used to the bungee-like sensation, but it still made me feel queasy. I opened my eyes and found myself near a small road in the countryside. There were mountains in the distance, clouds in the sky, and a field nearby.

A horse-drawn carriage went by, making a clattering sound as it did. I also saw a large tree somewhere in the distance. It was then that I realized I recognized this place.

I walked over to the trunk of the tree and placed my hand on it. It was exactly where I thought I was.

This was the place where I first opened my eyes in this world. This was where it all began.

That meant the carriage was probably headed to Reflet. As I took in the nostalgic feeling surrounding the place, my sister warped in not too far away.

"If you had landed back at the castle I would've given you an A+ grade! But... You made it back to the right world, you know? So you get a B-." ... *Geez.* I thought about something that made me grimace for a half-second, then asked Karen a question.

"...Would I be able to use this power to return to the world I was born in?"

"Umm... That world is pretty far down the chain, you know? It'd probably be hard to reach it as you are now. But you could when you get used to it. I just wouldn't suggest it..." *Yeah... Fair enough. If I showed up there after being dead for this long, that would cause issues.*

Guess I could turn invisible and take a look around, though... I decided that I'd definitely go back there someday, that day just wasn't coming any time soon.

As far as I was concerned, the world I stood in was my world. I didn't need any other.

"Can I take others with me to other worlds like this?"

"You can do that, you know? Just be careful… That toxic world we went to would've killed any of your fiancees, so don't jump to worlds you don't know!" That would've been bad. Without the divinity that we gods had, there was a chance I could've taken someone to a world where they would've just instantly died. That got me wondering how Ende dealt with that issue. He probably had the luxury of scoping out a world in the space between dimensions before actually going inside. *Come to think of it, I haven't heard from Ende… Wonder if he's okay. Then again, he's not the kind of guy who'd die easily or anything.*

"Actually that reminds me… That spirit world you took me to that one time, was that another world?"

"Not exactly, you know? It's more like an add-on to existing worlds. Kind of like a satellite that exists in its own bubble? If the main world was destroyed, the spirit realm that corresponded to it would also vanish, you know?"

That made sense. So the spirits would disappear along with the world… That got me wondering something else. "Wait, then… Doesn't the Reverse World have its own spirit realm? Wouldn't it get mixed with ours when the two worlds collide?"

"If the worlds were too far apart to start with then that would be possible, you know? But the Reverse world is a neighbor to this one, so they share the same spirit realm. But I don't really know how the spirits will react when the two worlds become one. There could be cases like extreme climate change, rising sea levels, or even displacement of landmasses, you know?"

"Wait a sec! Wait a sec! Don't just talk about something so serious in a casual tone! Why didn't you tell me that sooner?!" After my sudden outburst, Karen responded by staring at me blankly. Then she blinked once or twice, stuck out her tongue, and threw me a wink.

"…Oopsie!"

"Hello, God Almighty? There's a goddess down here who isn't doing a very good job of helping me! All she does is eat dessert, I'd like to swap her out for a better model."

"No waaaaaay!! Don't be mean, you know? I taught you how to move across worlds, you know?! I just forgot one teeny thiiiiiing!" I started faking a call to the old man, so Karen started whining and grabbing on to my side. *Geez… That isn't a teeny thing at all! If the new world ends up falling to ruin due to the spirits freaking out, it'd make me look like an idiot!*

"So how do we deal with it?"

"Umm… You could warn the spirits in advance so they aren't surprised when it happens? Or you could just make them your servants, you know? You have divinity and all."

That was right. The Sand Spirit I met in Sandora said something to that effect. That spirits were subservient to the power of the gods.

"Well, you aren't exactly a full god yet or anything, you know? There'll be some spirits that would take more convincing than others."

"So… how do I go about making spirits obey me?"

"There are countless methods, you know?

"Method 1! Persuasion!

"You gotta talk it out with the spirits and make them see your side of things, you know? It's a good, calm way out! Love and peace, you know?

"Method 2! Beat the crap outta them!

"Show them that they can't hope to match up to a god! Bully them into submission, you know? Might makes right! Search and destroy, you know?

And that's it."

"That's two methods! You said there were countless ones! Gaaah!"

So I have to talk or use force? This ain't right!

"Method three... Blackmail..."

"What..."

"Figure out their weakness, you know? That won't really make them obedient, though. They'll probably resist you and be upset. You gotta think about it like you're the new boss at a company, you know? Some employees will listen, while others will be more difficult. If you have the time, you can talk to them one by one and solve their issues, but if you don't have time, then..."

"Then it's method two..."

I need to take the search and destroy route? No way, any company doing that would go under! That'd be past shady dealings and going straight into criminal activity. I can't do this! This metaphor doesn't even really work!

"What's the problem with method two? Didn't you use that exact method to subdue Kohaku and the others?"

... Wasn't that different? No... I guess it wasn't, huh.

"If the spirit ends up being agreeable, then you can just leave them alone, you know? If the spirit is less agreeable, then just overpower it and it'll obey. Spirits are pretty honest like that." *Really? They won't hate me? I don't exactly want to be known as a spirit bully or anything. Is it really gonna be like an old TV drama where the two people disagreeing have a fistfight then come to a heartfelt understanding? I don't buy it.*

"For now all I need to do is go to the spirit realm, right?"

"That's right, you know? When you approach the spirit, tell them that you're the upcoming patron of this world and that they should listen to you even if it's a little annoying, you know? After

129

that, the spirits will probably divide into two groups, the ones who say "Sure!" and the ones who say "Heck no!" Then you just need to destroy the latter group, you know?" ...*Destroy? I don't wanna kill them! Sis, please don't be so overdramatic.*

Well, I do remember hearing that spirits couldn't strictly die and would eventually come back, so... I guess I don't need to hold back? I'd rather this went peacefully, though... The whole peace and love thing sounds nice.

But I'm pretty used to things not going how I want them to, so...

Guess it's time for some old-fashioned searching and destroying.

"Grooowraaauuugh!"

The giant Minotaur-like spirit staggered backward after I landed a solid punch on his snout.

He was either a spirit of copper or zinc, I couldn't remember. After I'd landed in the spirit realm and done exactly as Karen told me, they did just about what Karen expected. They split into two camps that either liked me or hated me. The ones that liked me were all like "Okay! We'll work with you!" while the ones that didn't like me were all like "Grr! Why would we obey someone like you, huh?!"

And that's how I came to be having a (fist-based) conversation with the rebellious spirits.

I activated my Apotheosis so I wouldn't get worn out, but they were surprisingly resilient. For example, this copper or zinc guy that I'd just beaten was a specific type of metal, and if you went up the chain of command he and his cohorts were dependents of the Stone Spirit.

I figured that if I could just get the Stone Spirit to join my side, then everyone in his family tree would be on my side as well.

But I was wrong. Even though I'd converted him to my side, they still fought back.

They just came up to me yelling stuff like "It doesn't matter if you convinced stone-bro! We're more than enough for a puny god like you!", and then when I beat one of them they were just like "Huh? Think you're hot shit cause you beat the Tin Spirit?! He was the weakest one of us!" It was annoying as heck.

"Woohoo! He did it! Mister Touya does it again!"

"Ahaha, rough 'em up! Kick their butts! You're so amazing, darling!"

"Serves you right, you big meanie! Show him who's boss, tough guy!" The spirits who had already pledged allegiance to me cheered loudly as they celebrated my upper hand. For whatever reason, most of the spirits that joined me identified as female, while the ones that went against me identified as male.

Thanks to that distinction, I felt like I just pissed off the guy ones even more... I didn't exactly feel good punching them out, either way.

There were a few female spirits among the rebellious ones, too. But they were more like rowdy delinquent girls... But still, spirit or not, I found it hard to hit girls, so I did end up pulling a few punches here and there.

And then after I beat them, for whatever reason or other, those defeated girls joined my crew and started cheering for me too.

"Oooh, lord Touyaaa! Go and win!"

"Do your best, sweetie!"

"Mm! I just wanna eat you up!" There were a few weird male spirits that I'd defeated and converted, as well... They were cheering for me... I didn't exactly want to be their friend, though.

"Come at me next, child!" Another shirtless, musclebound spirit came charging at me. He wore a turban and had Arabian-esque pants on.

"Stormy! You better not fight against Touya!"

"Ghh... Enough outta you! Even if you feel that way, Wind, I can't just accept him as my boss!" The Wind Spirit, clad in light green, frowned at her subordinate and berated him a little more. It seemed he was the Storm Spirit. He was supposed to listen to the Wind Spirit, but he just wasn't having it.

"Take this!" The Storm Spirit turned his legs into a swirling vortex as he charged toward me. His fist was sparking with lightning as he raised it, preparing to knock me down. But I simply raised Brunhild and shot him in the head with a divine bullet.

"Ow!" Given that something so powerful only made him say ow, that was a testament to how resilient spirits could be. The bullet was still just hardened rubber, but the divinity I'd clad it in would've been enough to obliterate most things.

Either way, his momentum was damaged, allowing me to punch him hard in the side. I'd enhanced it with **[Power Rise]**, too.

"Guuuuh!!" He flew backward and smacked into the Zinc Spirit that I'd defeated earlier.

What a pain all these spirits were. They were so single-minded that I was glad a good chunk of them had just joined my side off the bat.

"Woohoo! You're the best, Touya! Hey, Stormy! You're all thunder and no lightning! Give up already!"

The Wind Spirit went after the Storm Spirit and started slapping him about. *Hey now... He's part of your family, right? Be nicer! You're making the poor guy cry!*

There was a hierarchy in the spirit realm, apparently, with the pillar spirits standing at the top. They could be considered the representatives of all the other spirits.

Apparently, the Wind Spirit was one of these pillar spirits, but I had difficulty seeing her as something important. She was about as nonchalant as Karen was.

"Did you think something weird about me just now, you know?"

"I didn't." Karen was watching me fight, and she seemed sharp as ever. I just pretended like she was wrong, didn't have time to deal with her hassle.

Among the other pillar spirits, there was the Water Spirit, the Light Spirit, and the Earth Spirit. They'd all sided with me.

Interestingly enough, another of the pillar spirits was here. The Dark Spirit. The very same one I'd fought back in Ramissh.

She had revived and assumed her true form. She claimed to have not been in her right mind back during our last encounter.

The funniest thing about it to me was that she, who was once a monstrous beast with several appendages, now took the form of a young girl with black hair and black eyes.

She wore a black one-piece dress and shyly waved over toward me as she sat next to the Light Spirit. Her hair was in a short bob, and she almost looked like she was sitting with her older sister. The Light Spirit had curly, golden hair and a bright smile.

The Dark Spirit that I had fought back in Ramissh had taken that form after being contaminated with thousands of years of negative human emotions.

To be honest I felt kind of guilty knowing that I'd so mercilessly beaten someone who seemed so innocent now. But even though I did that, she harbored no ill will toward me.

It was possible that when a spirit died and rebirthed itself, the new one didn't have any memories of its old life. But I dared not ask her.

Even so, seeing her innocently waving at me just made my heart ache. *I'm really sorry... Please forgive me. I didn't know you were such a sweetheart!*

"Each and every one of you weaklings is a disappointment! Let me handle this!" A female spirit stepped forward. She had blazing red hair and quite literal sparks of fire in her eyes. She wore similar clothing to the Wind Spirit, but it was cut shorter for ease of movement.

"That's the Fire Spirit, you know?"

"Oh? A pillar spirit?"

"A pillar spirit."

Karen was pretty blunt about it. *Interesting... The Fire Spirit, eh? Does that mean all the pillar spirits are women?*

"Pillar spirits... Or rather, all spirits, go through a several-thousand-year life cycle. In the end, they revive themselves and are reborn. They can become a man or a woman, or even an animal, or something like a dragon, you know? It's just a coincidence that most of this generation identifies as female. Their personalities and emotions change based on the form they take, as well. That's how they can get the most varied life experience, you know?" *Huh... It's kinda hard to fight against a girl, though... But I think this one's the last female enemy.*

"Get a load of this!"

The Fire Spirit charged toward me, a loud sound ringing out with each step she took. She was generating explosions beneath her feet, intensifying her own speed with each inch closer to me. *Does she have dynamite in her soles or something?! Geez!*

"Haaah!"

She raised her hands and called forth several balls of fire. She cared not for her surroundings, reducing it all to a raging sea of flames. I was worried about the cheering spirits behind me, but the Water Spirit had already erected a protective barrier for them.

I flew into the sky of the spirit realm and dodged each of her shots. I didn't need to cast [Fly] when my Apotheosis was active.

"Don't think you can run...!" Suddenly, several pillars of flame came billowing up into the air. They then split apart and completely surrounded me, attempting to trap me in a pincer movement.

I quickly turned Brunhild into blade mode and slashed ahead, sending a wave of divinity to disperse the fire.

"How?!"

"How about I get a turn to attack, huh?!" The maximum speed I could reach during my Apotheosis was far faster than [Accel] and [Boost] combined. If I actually used this kind of power back down in the mortal realm, then I'd probably end up collapsing right away and going unconscious for a while... But the spirit realm was closer to the divine realm, so I wasn't drained as fast.

I moved toward the Fire Spirit in the blink of an eye. I grabbed both of her hands with one of mine, restraining her fully. I then took care not to injure her too badly before sweeping her leg out from under her, then I slammed her body into the ground.

"What?!" I pointed Brunhild's blade right at her chest. It was over.

"I... I lost..." I pulled up the Fire Spirit by the hand because she'd admitted I was the victor. For some reason, her face was reddish around the cheeks. I wondered if she was OK.

"Y-You're plenty strong, huh…"

"Hm? I guess so, yeah. I train against a sword demon every day." Even though I trained with Moroha daily, I didn't think I was even close to matching up to her ability. She was the god of swords, though… So in terms of technique, I was completely screwed by default. But I felt like in terms of general battle ability she was way above me, too.

"Alright. Who's next? You guys still want a piece of me?" I threw a few inflammatory comments toward the other rebellious spirits. I figured riling them up would make more of them attack me at once. I wanted it to be over already.

"W-Well… G-Good luck in your fights…! U-Umm… I'll be cheering for you… Gosh…"

"Hm? Oh, sure." The Fire Spirit emitted a few deep red flames for some reason and shuffled off awkwardly. I didn't know what was up with her.

She was completely red-faced up to her ears, and she was emitting a few reddish flames from her head. I wondered if she had a fever or something… It wouldn't be unusual for the Fire Spirit to have a high body temperature, but she didn't feel all that heated when I touched her arm.

Karen simply stared at me and looked frustrated for some reason. She let out a sigh and started muttering.

"…It might be because of your divinity stemming from the highest tier of godhood, but you really are a natural ladykiller… I fear for the future, you know?"

"What are you talking about? I'm not a killer…"

What does she mean? I try to avoid fatalities whenever I can!

I sighed quietly and turned back to the other spirits, before suddenly realizing that they were directing raw killing intent in my direction. *Wait, what?! Did my insult just now work or something?*

"You piece of shit…! You took away our precious fire!"

"I-I'm so jealous! What the hell?! I'm so damn jealous! First, you run off with Dark, and now you want Fire to yourself, too?!"

"Today I will kill a god!"

"Even if you took away the flame of our Fire Spirit, the embers of envy in my soul are heating up!" *Huh? What…? Why are they crying? Wait… Why are their tears red?! Spirits are so damn weird!*

"Death to the enemy!"

"Chaaaarge!" The remaining spirits all cried out in rage, and what sounded like misery, before charging toward me. *Why are you crying?! What did I do?!* A short while later, the spirits were scattered across the battlefield. They were completely defeated.

For some reason, I felt guilty… It was almost like I was the villain here for whatever reason.

"Hgh… I have no regrets… Even if I knew we'd lose, I still had to stand and fight for what was right…"

"The embers of my envy will never fade… Someday we'll get that bastard… Someday…"

"Ahh… Th-The Dark Spirit is such a hottie… Unf…" A few of them were muttering things I really preferred to just ignore.

The Light Spirit stepped forward from the crowd and looked over to me. She raised her hand into the air and began speaking loudly.

"We, the pillar spirits declare our recognition of the Celestial Spirit King, Mochizuki Touya. It is our hope that he will guide us well into the future." The Water, Earth, Fire, Wind, and Dark Spirits raised their hands into the air and joined the spirit of light in their pledge.

And with that, the issue with the spirits was resolved. It ended up getting pretty rowdy, but it was all over now.

Even so, I couldn't help but wonder if there wasn't a better way…

◇　◇　◇

"So what's the deal with Ancient Spirit Magic, exactly?" I sat around in the glimmering spirit realm and asked the pillar spirits a question.

We were having a small tea party. I'd pulled a table and chairs out of [Storage], along with some tea and snacks.

It was kind of a weird sensation, since the spirit realm didn't actually have a ground or anything, so we were floating but not at the same time. It was even weirder because the Storm Spirit I'd beaten up earlier had totally rolled around as if hitting the ground when I knocked him over. I didn't understand the rules at all.

"You know? That whole Ancient Spirit Magic thing?" Belfast's court magician, Charlotte, was researching that if I recalled correctly. I hadn't gone to visit her in a while, though.

"That is magic forged through contracts. We lend our powers to those who bind a contract with us. But the proper way to form those contracts is no longer around in the mortal realm. It would appear that our language, the Ancient Spirit Script, has also been lost."

"There were times when our spiritual dependents could be called out by mistake, but none of the people down there actually understood enough to see what they were messing with. In the end, they just kept asking for power, and nobody managed to form a proper contract." The Fire and Light Spirits answered my question.

It seemed that to contract with a spirit, you needed to form a mutual arrangement. You were borrowing power from them, after all. Which meant you had to see them as equals.

It was different from summoning a beast, as well. Spirits were allowed to break the contract if they were unsatisfied. If they were asked to do something they didn't want to do, they were also allowed to refuse.

If summoned beasts were like employees or laborers, then spirits were more like friends. If you treated your friends like workers, then they'd obviously get fed up with you and leave.

Then again, if you kept pushing your employees they'd probably get upset with you as well.

"So I guess I should start spreading a more spirit-friendly agenda, huh? I guess I should talk about how spirits are equal to humanity."

"Actually it might be troubling if we were contracted and then relied on too much. We wouldn't want our contractors becoming too familiar with us, either." The Earth spirit folded her arms.

Spirits were basically personifications of natural elements. Since the olden days, people have revered mountains, worshiped the seas, feared foul winds, and thanked the earth for its bounty. That was why spirits were indispensable to the gods and went on to form the worlds they were assigned to.

"Well, putting you guys aside for a minute, Spirit magic should be usable by contracting with your dependents, right?"

"That's right. Take one of mine, for example, a Salamander. If you formed a contract with one, then you'd be able to use Fire Spirit magic."

The Fire Spirit shrugged as she ate a cookie. It seemed like the magic's power depended entirely on the skill of the contractor.

Normal magic required you to have an aptitude in that particular element. The elements of fire, water, light, earth, wind, dark, and null. If you didn't have an aptitude for one, you wouldn't be able to use magic.

However, Spirit magic could actually be used by anyone that managed to contract for it. But there were also some prerequisites to being able to forge a contract, so I couldn't exactly say if it was easier or not.

This probably sounded obvious, but someone with an aptitude for Water magic was more likely to get along with a water-related spirit. It wasn't too hard to realize why the use of Spirit magic fell into decline over time, given that kind of preferential treatment.

If someone was capable of using Water magic and had to choose between using their own or asking a spirit to lend them their power to do something similar... It's obvious that most people would just use their own Water spells.

But Spirit magic had its own perks. For example, no matter how big the scale of the spell, it had minimal impact on the caster's own mana reserves.

That was pretty obvious, though. The one who actually used the magic was the spirit being summoned. All the summoner had to do was use enough magic to call the spirit.

So even a little child with a small amount of magic could potentially cast devastating spells by becoming friends with a more powerful spirit.

That was why it was important to manage the world's understanding of spirits and their nature.

The pillar spirits all agreed that my proposal of spreading Spirit magic throughout the world again was fine. Obviously, the details of contracting would be up to the individual spirits. It's not like they had to do anything they didn't want to do. That's what separated this from a mere summoning ritual. The spirits and the contractors were on equal footing.

Some of the rebellious spirits got angry at the idea, and declared that "We'll never contract with anyone married, or anyone with a girlfriend! I'm not lending my power to any Chads, they have it good as it is!" Frankly, they were weirding me out, so I just let them stew in it. They had freedom of choice at the end of the day.

I didn't really understand them, or why they were making paper masks with the word "Envy" written on them, but I just decided to leave it be.

"The main issue is most people can't see spirits, I guess."

"Once a spirit gets recognized, then we'll always be visible. Fairies should be able to see us pretty easily, too. There are also humans out there with a rare birth condition that gives them spirit sight!"

The Wind Spirit had a point, the fairies would definitely be able to master Spirit magic pretty easily. They were practically pros at regular magic anyway.

I decided to go find Charlotte and talk to her about it. She knew the most about Spirit magic out of anyone that I knew.

◇   ◇   ◇

"...Wh-What was that?" I was in Belfast's magical research division, talking to Charlotte. What I'd just asked her caused her to stare in disbelief and drop some of her papers on the floor.

"Like I said, would you like me to show you how to use Spirit magic?"

"H-Huh? What? P-Please slow down... Spirit magic? Touya... Er, Grand Duke... Are you telling me you can use it?"

"Yeah, look at this." I called out a spirit from the wind family, Sylph. She was a tiny girl about the size of a pixie. I brought her out specifically so that Charlotte could easily get a grasp of what a spirit was like.

"Why is this happening?! Why can you use it all of a sudden?! I dedicated my life to studying it and... And you just show up and use it?!"

141

"...A-Ah... Sorry..." The genius woman in front of me immediately broke down like a child. It seemed my casual way of doing it was a little insensitive.

Charlotte's assistants came over to calm her down. Her assistants seemed to be wearing copies of the translation glasses I'd given to Charlotte forever ago.

After a while, Charlotte stopped bawling and regained her composure. She started asking me questions while staring at the Sylph.

"It's a spirit... A real one... You know, when I was a little girl I actually saw a spirit once. That's why I wanted to research Spirit magic to begin with! I'm a little sad it's through your power and not mine, but I'm really happy to see another after so long..."

That was interesting. I never knew why Charlotte had started her studying to begin with.

"I've made an agreement with the elemental pillar spirits, the ones that are far higher in rank than this little one. We'd like to spread Spirit magic across the world again. Would you help us, Charlotte?!"

"I'll help! I'll help! I'llhelpI'llhelpI'llhelp!!!"

Charlotte leaned in close and started flailing madly. *Easy there, Charlotte! Your words are breaking apart.*

The other researchers calmed her down again and I started to write the fundamentals of Spirit magic down on a nearby blackboard. I almost felt like a school teacher.

"So, there are pillar spirits, then specialized spirits under each of those, and then a tier below that are the dependents, creatures within an elemental family. Pillar spirits pretty much never make contracts with humans, so Spirit magic is usually achieved by contracting with a specialized spirit or an elemental dependent... I'll call those ones lesser spirits. Anyway, you need to form a contract with a lesser spirit or a specialized spirit to use Spirit magic." Charlotte and the others jotted down my words into their notebooks.

"The most important thing to remember when contracting with a spirit is that they are not summoned beasts. You are to stand on equal footing with them, and treat them that way. Ultimately, what'll count when it comes to being a good contractor or not, is your capacity to see spirits as potential friends." I was the Celestial Spirit King now, so I didn't need to worry about forging any contracts individually, all spirits naturally obeyed me.

It would also be impossible to use Spirit magic against me, as no spirit would dare try to harm me.

...Well, I did have my doubts about that point. Those crying guys came to mind, for one. But it was better not to worry about it.

"Spirits typically cannot be noticed or seen, but they're in the world around us. If you want to speak with spirits, then you need to be versed in spirit tongue. If you try speaking in that language, then they should reveal their form to you."

"Oh! Is that the same as Ancient Spirit Script?"

"It's similar, but not quite the same. Ancient Spirit Script was like a derivative language made in ancient times. The proper meaning of the words probably wouldn't get through to the spirits if you tried speaking that language." The pillar spirits and most of the specialized spirits did speak the common tongue, however.

I took out a book from [Storage]. The title was "True Spirit Tongue." It was an instructional linguistic manual I'd made in Babylon's workshop, with the help of a few spirits.

"If you read this, you should be able to have a conversation with a spirit. I'll let you have it."

"A-Are you sure that's okay?"

"It's just fine. In exchange, I'd like you guys to make a public effort toward getting people friendly with spirits. It's important that humanity and spiritkind get along, things are going to happen in the future that makes it a necessity." When the worlds combined, the spirits would find their jobs stretched, and there'd be trouble. Natural disasters and ecological changes were highly likely to happen.

As the Celestial Spirit King, I'd granted some of my divine power to the spirits in order to strengthen them for the time being. But that wouldn't last too long into the future, so the people of both worlds needed to form lasting bonds with the spirits in order to increase their power.

That's what Karen told me, at least. It wouldn't be super relevant for a while, but it was important to plant the seeds.

But if I was going to manage the new world that this place would eventually become, I had to get it handled.

Spirit magic definitely wasn't used in the Reverse World, either. So it was likely that the art was completely lost over there, too.

There were surely spirits doing stuff over there as well, but their contact with humans seemed to be minimal. That's why I decided to focus on cultivating the relationship in just this world for now.

"So, shall we test out whether you can form a contract? Charlotte, what magic schools did you have an aptitude for, again?"

"Um... I have five. Everything except dark and null." Five was pretty impressive... Leen had six, and she was a fairy. Charlotte was clearly an exemplary human, it seemed she wasn't the court magician for no reason.

"It's your first time, so you'll probably call on a Lesser Water or Wind Spirit. The spirits of the wind family are all naturally curious, and the water family is made up of gentle and calm spirits, so they're the easiest to contract with."

"Okay… I'll try to call out a Lesser Water Spirit, then." We went outside and walked toward the fountain in the courtyard.

Calling a spirit for the first time required the proper medium. In the case of a Lesser Water Spirit, all you really needed was a body of water.

Charlotte took out the book I'd given her and started reading out the passage about water summoning.

After she spoke, the water from the fountain stopped flowing, coming together in mid-air to take the form of a Lesser Water Spirit. She was an Undine. As small as the Sylph, except she had a mermaid tail instead of legs.

Charlotte was completely flustered at the sight, leading the Undine to just stare at her.

"Hey, don't forget the contract."

"A-A-Ah, yes! U-Uhm…!" Charlotte shakily flipped through the pages and began to awkwardly speak the spirit tongue.

If one were to translate it into common, it would be something along the lines of "Oh spirit, I'd love it if we could become closer. I would love to become your friend. Please take a chance on my humble self." Or something like that.

Contracting with a spirit was more about what was felt than what was said, really. Even if Charlotte had said it fluently, if she didn't mean it then her feelings wouldn't impact the spirit at all. In a way that was similar to humans, you could typically tell when someone really meant something.

The Undine floated in the air for a little bit before swimming forward, smiling, and touching Charlotte's hand.

She then swam through the air, completing a few laps around Charlotte before landing on top of her hand again and vanishing in a flash of light.

The flash gave way to a tiny blue crystal in Charlotte's hand.

"Um... Grand Duke? What's this?"

"Good work. You formed the contract, she likes you. This is a spiritual stone. It's basically the proof of your contract. If you ever need her, hold the stone in your hand and call out for her."

"O-Okay!" Charlotte closed her eyes and held the spiritual stone close to her bosom. As if reacting to the silent call, the Undine jumped out of the fountain and began to swim circles around Charlotte again.

"It'll be tougher to call her out somewhere without much water because she needs a certain amount to manifest her form. But you should be able to manage so long as you have a cup's worth or so. What she can do for you depends on how much your friendship progresses."

"O-Okay! I'll do my best!" Charlotte giggled as she played around with the Undine. Her research assistants then attempted their own contracts, calling forth another Undine and a Sylph.

"Those spiritual stones should be kept on hand, though. Don't lose them. You can probably attach them to a ring or a pendant, just try not to damage the stones when you do that." They weren't really listening, they were just playing around happily with their spirits. I guess it was understandable, though. They'd basically fulfilled a lifelong dream.

"What's all this, then?" The king of Belfast came out into the courtyard. Queen Yuel trailed behind him, carrying little Prince Yamato in her arms.

I told them that I'd taught Charlotte and the others how to use Spirit magic, prompting stares of disbelief. Then they just shook their heads, sighed, and said nothing about me could really surprise them at this point.

I had planned on giving out copies of the book to other countries as well.

Charlotte and the others left with their spirits, seemingly excited to go and play back in the lab. I was pleased for them.

"Wow... Yamato sure got bigger!" I looked over at the infant in Yuel's arms, prompting his father to give a broad grin.

"That's right, my boy! He's a happy, healthy lad! Check out these photos I took earlier, here! Take a look!"

The king took out his smartphone and started cycling through an entire album of baby pictures. He... certainly seemed enthusiastic. I was almost getting Xenoahs Overlord vibes.

I could understand his excitement since he seemed like he'd always wanted a son, but I wondered if he planned on keeping photographic evidence of every day of Yamato's life.

...I wonder if I'll be that kind of dad. Hopefully, I learn from these old coots and don't make the same mista— Hhgh...!

...What the... What was that feeling just now...? Did it come from the queen? No... It's coming from Yamato?

I felt something strange emanating from the little prince, like a pulsing heartbeat. I asked if I could carry him for a moment. His magic power was fairly standard... He seemed healthy... But something about him felt *wrong* all of a sudden.

The cooing baby rolled around in my arms, happily playing. I decided to channel some of my divinity into my eyes and use my divine sight to see if that would help identify what was throwing me off. When I did... I saw something that made my blood run cold.

My entire body shook, and I handed the prince back to his mother.

"Something wrong, Touya? You look a little frazzled."

"Huh? Oh... N-Nothing... I was just... Just a bit scared since I didn't want to drop him."

"Pfft, don't be ridiculous my lad! How are you gonna cope when you and Yumina have a baby, eh? You better get used to it now before it bites you in the butt later!" The king laughed out loud, but I couldn't force myself to join in. I was torn on whether or not to tell him what I had just discovered.

My divine sight had revealed something. A physical abnormality inside the prince's heart. I... I couldn't deny what I had seen. A Phrase Core.

Within that boy's body was the entity that an entire species had been hunting. An entity that caused untold bloodshed across countless worlds. Prince Yamato was an unwitting host, being fed on by the Sovereign Phrase.

◇　◇　◇

"No way..."

I told Yumina and my other fiancees about the situation with Prince Yamato. I didn't have enough courage to tell the king and queen of Belfast.

After she heard me out, Yumina simply slumped down on my bed. Her face was pale.

"...Is... Is there nothing we can do?"

"Well... We could do something. Since I used divinity to see it, I could probably use [**Apport**] in my Apotheosis form to pull it out of him. It's possible that might cause some internal bleeding, but if we had recovery magic ready immediately, he'd be okay... There's just one problem." The girls looked at me expectantly. This was a serious issue, so I decided to just say it.

"The moment I take that core out of Yamato's body, an army of Phrase will likely emerge in the vicinity. At the very least, that's what I expect. That's why we'd have to do it somewhere where we could mitigate the damage… Like the ruins of Yulong." The Sovereign was hiding itself using Prince Yamato's heartbeat. If that cover was removed, then every Phrase across all reality would immediately be able to zero in on the Sovereign's signature. They'd end up crashing against the world barrier, and would probably draw some mutants in for good measure.

"Can we not destroy the core the moment it is removed, can we not?"

"I doubt it could be destroyed so easily. And frankly, I want to avoid destroying it. That would cause us major trouble." Ende would become our enemy if I did that. He wouldn't ever forgive me for murdering the person he loved.

I wouldn't be surprised if he ended up killing Yumina and the others, one by one, to give me a taste of his grief. That's what I'd do in his situation at least.

There was also that one female Dominant Construct, Ney. She was loyal to the Sovereign, so she'd definitely try to avenge her. Well, we were enemies to begin with so nothing much would actually change there.

"Then what do we do?! We can't just keep the core inside Yamato!"

"Please calm down, Yumina. I have an idea… Look at this spell, first." I reached out my hand and pointed it toward the table in my room. Then, I triggered a spell I'd learned from one of the books that Palerius had left behind.

"[Prison]."

A blue-hued white cube suddenly surrounded the table and began shrinking. It kept on reducing in size until it was around three centimeters in diameter.

"This is my Null spell, [Prison]. It can seal anything inside it regardless of whether it's living or dead. It's like a Space-time spell coupled with a sealing spell, basically. The power of this prison is also charged with my divinity, meaning that nothing could get in from the outside. Not unless it was a god at least. It also makes it the perfect safety bunker." It was different from **Storage** in that it still occupied physical space, and could trap living beings inside.

The tiny die-sized cube was partially see-through, so everyone could plainly see the tiny table trapped within.

I was capable of altering the size of the prison, and everything inside it would shrink proportionally. It was basically an inescapable jail or an impenetrable shelter.

I could even tweak it so only certain things could pass through. For example, I could prevent the flow of air through the space, forcing the person to choke to death inside, or I could allow it so cooked meals and water could pass through, so anyone I kept trapped would be fed and watered. I could even tweak it so only one sex could pass through. Blocking all males from entering and making it a female-only space, for example.

The only trade-off to this tweaking was that the larger the prison, the weaker the effect it had.

"[Release]."

The moment I said that, the die shattered to bits and vanished, causing the table to reappear where it was, in its complete original size.

"There are different methods you can set to open the prison, too. If we take the Sovereign Core and put it in here when we get it out, we should be okay." Everyone sighed in relief. Even Yumina seemed appeased by this answer.

Using my new spell, we'd be able to make sure Prince Yamato was okay.

But the real question would be what to do with the core when we had it.

If the Phrase were after it, there was always the option of just handing it over to them and hoping they'd retreat.

But it wasn't like the Mutated Constructs would leave if we did that. They were completely following the wicked god, after all. In the worst case scenario, the wicked god's group would steal away the core from the Phrase after I handed it over to them. I really didn't want to make a situation where the wicked god grew any stronger.

There was always the option of just handing it over to Ende. After that, he'd take the core with him to another world, and the Phrase would follow. That would ensure they'd leave this world alone, but the wicked god would still be an issue.

Plus, I wasn't too keen on the idea of just forcing the issue away on to another world.

"That's not something a future world patron should be doing…" I sighed quietly and decided that using [**Prison**] on the core and figuring it out later was the best course of action.

I needed to speak with the king of Belfast, and his wife. I could hardly do anything to their little boy without warning them beforehand. I didn't really want to admit it, but there was a tiny chance something could go wrong in the extraction… I didn't want to risk anything without them knowing.

I let out a small sigh. I really didn't know what to tell them…

"What do you mean?! Does this mean the Phrase were trying to kill my son this entire time?!"

"Not exactly, no. The Phrase have no idea that their target is inside him. But once they are aware, they'd definitely target him." If I had to make a guess of it, it was a case of bad timing. The Sovereign's previous host must have died around the same time Prince Yamato was born. According to Ende, the new host was typically selected at random, so this was all just a terrible coincidence.

Queen Yuel was visibly shaken; she held her infant close. Just to be sure, I'd cast [**Prison**] around the room we were in, in order to prevent any outsiders from listening to this sensitive information. The only people in here were Yumina, myself, Yamato, and their parents. As far as I knew, the only thing other than myself capable of breaking down the [**Prison**] would be the wicked god itself.

"Father, please calm yourself. Touya can remove the core from Yamato. We just came here because we obviously couldn't do such a thing without your consent. Please understand."

"I-Is that truly the case? Then... You can save my boy?"

"Well, to be honest, even if we left the core inside of him he'd grow up healthy and happy. There's nothing indicating that the Sovereign has any negative effects on him. But it would be better to remove it. Even so, I can't guarantee that he won't be completely unharmed by the procedure... Is that still okay?" He was still a baby, so his parents had final say. I didn't even want to consider the worst case scenario, but I felt like they deserved my honesty.

The king of Belfast stared into my eyes, and slowly he spoke.

"...Very well. We ask that you do it. Little Yamato is in your hands, Touya."

"Very well... In that case..." I disabled the barrier around us and opened a portal to a barren wasteland in the middle of Yulong. This might've been seen as an overreaction, but I didn't want to take any chances. If the Sovereign's signal was released in Belfast, that could have spelled disaster for the entire nation.

I then activated [**Prison**] once more, sealing the five of us inside. The protections around the box would hopefully prevent the Phrase from immediately noticing the Sovereign.

"I'm gonna do it, then." I channeled my divine sight and looked toward the sleeping prince. I clearly saw it, hidden in a tiny corner of the boy's heart. It was a tiny, regular icosahedron, about the size of a cherry. *Alright... That should be exactly where it is... Now or never...*

"[**Apport**]."

The tiny crystal then appeared in my right hand. I quickly used my left hand to apply Healing magic to the baby, while using my divine sight to check the inside of his body for any abnormalities. There weren't any. I decided to cast [**Recovery**] as well, just to be safe.

I let out a sigh as relief washed over me. The baby just cooed and babbled as if nothing had happened.

"Okay, it's fine now. I got it out."

"You did?! Amazing! You hear that, Yamato?" The king ran toward his son and gently grabbed the little guy by the hands, running his fingers over them. He looked like he was on the verge of tears. Queen Yuel and Yumina also had teary eyes. I was glad everything went okay.

Whew, that was actually way easier than I thought. Guess I got worried about nothing!

Now all I had to do was handle the Sovereign Core, and everything would be fine.

"Wh... What?!"

Or so I thought. When I opened up my closed palm to look at the crystal, it was transforming... Or rather, growing.

Crystal structures began to spread out from the core like icy outcroppings, rapidly expanding. I threw it to the ground before it took hold of my hand.

"Touya... What is happening?!"

"I think the Sovereign is waking up?! Either way, this is bad news!" I couldn't release the [**Prison**] or the Phrase would immediately discover our location.

I had no other option. I changed the settings of the box to remove Yuel, Yumina, Yamato, and the king from it, then warped them back to Belfast through a portal. I stayed alone just outside the box, watching the crystal structure continue to grow inside.

The crystal lump in front of me was already the size of a small child, and it wasn't slowing down. Gradually I could see nuance in its form, and it began to take the shape of a humanoid body.

It was a female, with soft curves. Crystal material wrapped around her and took the form of a regal dress. She had long hair that draped down past her shoulders.

The transformation was almost complete. What was standing in front of me was a feminine Dominant Construct. She looked about my age. The dress she wore sparkled as a dull white-blue light emanated from her body.

I'd seen a few Dominant Constructs so far, but none of them had nearly as much elegance and poise as this one. She was the very picture of royal grace.

Her eyes, an icy blue, slowly opened up.

She blinked once or twice, then stared at me. Eventually, she seemed to register me as another lifeform and opened her mouth.

Her mouth moved, but I heard nothing. That was my fault, though. The [**Prison**] I'd erected was soundproof.

The Sovereign noticed that I hadn't reacted to her words, so she just tilted her head, and then shrugged. She didn't seem hostile, at least.

"...If I remember right, Ende said she isn't much of a fighter." I worked up my resolve and took a step inside.

As I got closer, I couldn't help but notice the girl was a little nervous as well. She fidgeted with her hands before trying to speak again.

「@#……@$n/※o、#h@jimem@◇sh⊇i＊t≒e」

What? What is she saying…? Oh, right… She does come from another world entirely. Ney and Gila used words like that one, if I recall…-

I could use the [**Translation**] spell to give her knowledge of my language, but that required physical contact.

I didn't know if the Phrase understood the cultural importance of a handshake, but I held my arm out anyway.

She seemed wary of me, so I smiled to show her I wasn't hostile. That might've worried her more, given my smile was kinda forced.

Somehow my gesture worked because she reached out and grabbed my hand with both of hers. Her hand was cold, but definitely soft.

"[**Translation**]."

I quickly activated my translation magic, passing my own magic power through her hands, creating a neural link that should've triggered a shared recognition.

"Can you understand me now?"

"Hm?! I… Yes. Yes, I can." The Sovereign, with a shocked expression on her face, slowly began to talk. I was glad that the spell worked.

"I'm Mochizuki Touya. I am a grand duke, and I rule over one of the countries in this world."

"…Oh… Then I do beg your forgiveness. It seems an introduction is in order on my part. My name is Melle. I am the Sovereign Phrase, former world leader of Phrasia, a far-off Crystal Planet."

There was no doubt about it. She was the one they were looking for, standing right in front of me.

The Sovereign.

◇ ◇ ◇

"How'd it go?"

"No good. She didn't react to me at all, she's just despondent." The Phrase Sovereign, Melle, was currently in Babylon. She was living inside the Rampart castle.

This might've seemed a little rash, but we were currently keeping her confined. Her castle room was closed off by a [**Prison**], preventing her from leaving, and preventing the Phrase from detecting her.

The [**Prison**] was imbued with my own divinity so it wouldn't fade away even if I went to the Reverse World. It was basically a shelter with no entry or exit points for anyone I didn't want to have them.

I wasn't really worried about her escaping, though. I was more worried about her mental health.

After I met her, I told Melle the whole story of her people up until that point.

I told her about how a faction that didn't follow the new Sovereign splintered off from Phrasia, composed of the individuals she'd left behind to govern the place. About how they'd also gained the ability to cross through worlds.

About how they had committed genocide on countless worlds, all in the pursuit of either claiming Melle's power or to bring her home.

About how Ende and Lycee had been crossing worlds along with her, keeping a secret eye on her.

And about how, after arriving in this world, the Phrase known as Yula gained a new power, and used it to corrupt members of his own species to a new goal.

When I finished my story, I noticed that Melle looked utterly horrified, and it seemed the psychological toll on her was far too great. She became despondent due to shock.

She was a Phrase, so it wasn't like she'd die if she didn't eat or drink, but seeing her in that state made me think I'd said too much, too harshly. Nah, scratch that. I'd absolutely said too much, too harshly.

"Where are you, Ende... It'd be really nice if this was one of those moments you'd pop up out of nowhere like you usually do..." Ende wasn't showing up on any of the maps when I used my searching magic; he was probably in the gap between worlds or something.

It wasn't like all of this was Melle's fault, but it was true that it originated from her actions. I didn't want to tell her that this was her burden to shoulder alone, or that she needed to pay me reparations for the grief she caused, but it was still undeniable that countless people had been murdered by the Phrase.

To be honest, though, the ones that were directly responsible for this mess were the stalkers that had been trailing her this whole time.

If it were possible, I'd want her to persuade the Phrase to leave this world alone, along with other worlds too. She'd completely revived from the Sovereign Core, so it wasn't impossible.

But if she continued to sit there, depressed and unresponsive, it didn't seem like a likely course of action...

"Touya... What do you plan to do with her?" Yumina frowned gently. I'd told the king and queen of Belfast that I'd successfully sealed away the Sovereign. That wasn't exactly a lie, to be fair.

"What do you think, Yumina? The Phrase race is our enemy, right? Should I kill her? Should I seal her away somewhere forever?" I asked her a question that had a bit of a harsh tone to it, but I didn't want to seem like I hadn't been thinking about the hard stuff. I needed to figure out what to do with Melle.

I valued Yumina's insight, too.

"I... I think I understand how she might be feeling. I fell in love with someone from another world, as well. I think in her case... She was desperate. Desperate not to be separated from her beloved. She became so engrossed in being with him that she failed to see the bigger picture. She lost sight of what it would do to her people. I think that while the situation is tragic right now, it's not like we can't fix it."

Yumina reached out and grabbed my hand as she spoke. I looked at her face, and she softly smiled. Her mismatched eyes stared back up into mine.

"She came here on a path that caused chaos in its wake, that much is true. But you can help her, Touya... I'd like to see you try."

"Alright. I'll try my best, then."

"Please do, Touya... It goes without saying that we'll support you, too." I smiled at Yumina, but couldn't help but think she'd seen right through me. She really did have me wrapped around her little finger. Part of me worried I wouldn't be wearing the proverbial household pants much in the future. Well... It wasn't like I didn't already know that.

I wondered if I'd make a good god if I couldn't even make a call as simple as that without help.

"Oh, also... If you see Ende, please give him a stern talking to at the very least. A man can't just leave his beloved alone to suffer like this... That's no good at all! Actually, hit him for me."

"...I don't know if it's as simple as him just bailing on her." Yumina's reaction was understandable from her perspective, but it wasn't really fair. It wasn't like Ende knew she was here, and that was partially my fault.

That being said, I was a little annoyed at him for other reasons, so maybe smacking him around a bit would help me work through some stress.

Either way, Melle was in the care of Liora for the time being.

I'd used [**Program**] and my own divinity to create special restraints and instructed Liora to use them to hold Melle back if she attempted to commit suicide. But I hoped it wouldn't come to that.

There wasn't much more we could do with her for the time being, at any rate. I just had to hope she'd get better in the future.

My business with the spirits was concluded, too. If the two worlds ended up coming together, which they likely would, then there wouldn't be any major environmental issues.

There were still a couple of issues, so I headed out to the farmland to speak with uncle Kousuke. Of all the gods in Brunhild, I trusted his words the most.

It wasn't like the other gods weren't trustworthy, but he was the most down to earth.

"Well, it ain't like the worlds're gonna overlap on each other or somethin'. They'll just be connected an' right next to each other. Probably accessible by the sea." Kousuke took off his garden gloves and laid them down neatly as he spoke. He set them side by side as if to demonstrate a point.

I see... So none of the landmasses will actually touch, they'll just be in parallel, and accessible to everyone.

"If it wasn't fer that wicked god feller, it'd just be brushed off as suddenly discoverin' a new continent... Well, I guess it'd be hard to explain why the landmass was an exact mirror image."

"So... You think it might not be as confusing and catastrophic as it could be?"

"Sure... But that'd only be if there weren't a wicked god about. See... Once the merge goes ahead an' happens, the world ain't gonna be under the old man's protection no more. The wicked god an' its ilk are gonna be able to pour through without much stoppin' them." There'd be a mass attack from the Mutated Constructs. At the very least we'd be able to use Melle to keep the regular Phrase at bay.

The Mutated Constructs made themselves stronger by absorbing the regular ones, so it'd be better to have them clear out as soon as possible.

"Well, I wouldn't worry much if I were you, son. If you think yer gonna shoulder this all alone, that's the only thing that'd be yer downfall. Think about it. You planted plenty of seeds in this world. Seeds of hope an' trust. Now they've grown up, an' will bear fruit. The wicked god won't have an easy time fightin' you, I'm sure." I was happy to hear that from Kousuke. He was pretty wise and worldly, but I guess he was a down-to-earth kind of god. I wished that the annoying drunk and the chatty love goddess had more of his insight.

"Still... I am a teeny bit worried. Y'think the folks in that there Reverse World can defend themselves from the Phrase and the other ones? Those Gollems good enough at fightin'?"

"Well, there are some Gollems that can defeat them, I think. I'm not sure overall, though..."

I hadn't really thought about it. The crowns and certain other Gollems would be able to beat Mutated Constructs, but if an Upper Construct somehow got into the mix, I wasn't sure if they'd be able to win. With that in mind, I decided to head to the Reverse World and see if I could arrange more allies.

In terms of Reverse World allies, I had the Red Cats... And there was also Elluka, the Gollem Technologist. There was also her Gollem companion, Fenrir.

She was apparently a one-in-a-million genius in that world... At least that's what I'd been told. I had some serious reservations about how good she actually was when I remembered how silly she looked with those thick glasses, messy hair, and tattered clothing.

"Didja think've somethin'?"

"I think so, yeah."

"Then get yer ass goin'. No rush, but sittin' around won't fix anythin' either. Crops ain't gonna grow without gettin' watered."

He was right. I decided to go to the Reverse World and try to explain the situation to Elluka. She probably knew about Gollems with the right kind of power we needed, anyway.

"Alright, I'm heading off."

"See ya when I see ya. Good bounty to you."

Uncle Kousuke took up his sickle and headed back to work. I was about to engage my divinity and travel to the Reverse World, but I stopped myself. I decided to quickly head back to the castle and tell my fiancees where I was going. I didn't want them to worry, after all... I'd been doing that too much.

Still, it was possible that they'd ask me to take them with me...

"Are you ready?"

"A-Are we gonna be fine? We won't come out anywhere weird, will we?"

"It'll be fine, relax." I laughed softly toward Elze. She was usually so hot-headed, but she could be surprisingly cautious at times. Still, that was part of what made her cute.

This time Elze, Yae, and Hilde were coming with me. That was to make up for the fact that they didn't come last time.

Sue and Sakura were busy, so I promised to take them later.

This time we were going not through the dimensional disruptor, but through my own divinity.

According to Karen, I needed to be careful to only leap into worlds that I knew were safe for the people coming with me, or else I ran the risk of putting them in danger.

"Uhm... Just holding my hand is fine enough, you know..."

"N-No, Touya-dono... I just want to be safe, I do."

"That's right! This is much safer!" Hilde and Yae were tightly clinging to my left and right sides, while Elze was clinging on to me with a hug from the front. It was nice, but I still felt a little shy. I decided to quickly take us all to the Reverse World.

"A-Alright, let's do it." I blushed as I let my own divinity flow through me, gently enveloping the girls by my side with it as well... Then, we leaped into space-time itself.

◇   ◇   ◇

We ended up on a hillside overlooking a forest. There were some mountains in the distance. There were also a settlement and a few roads nearby, but it didn't look all that busy. It seemed like we were on some kind of frontier.

"I wanted to warp us to Allen, but I guess I missed my mark a bit…" I checked my map and found we were quite far off the mark. We were still within the Allent Theocracy, but nowhere near the capital city, Allen.

"It really doesn't seem like another world out here… Just looks like any other countryside." Elze gazed along the highway and muttered quietly. I felt the same way when I was reborn for the first time.

"These worlds run in parallel, so they aren't too different in terms of general terrain. Anyway… Elluka… Let's see here…" I searched for her on my smartphone map. She seemed to be north of Allen city.

I decided to stop by the capital using [Gate], and then use [Fly] to get the rest of the way afterward.

"We haven't had lunch yet. Do you guys wanna stop by in the capital?"

"That sounds good to me, it does. I would like to have something to eat, I would." Yae and the others seemed to get pretty excited at the prospect of lunch, so I fired up a [Gate] and took us to the city. Before we settled in at the cafe I'd gone to last time, I picked up another newspaper. The headline on the front page quickly caught my eye.

It said, "Golden Monsters Appear Once More." It looked like the Mutated Constructs had appeared in the Reverse World again. In Allen City, no less.

Apparently, the battle Gollems and the templar knights of the kingdom managed to fend them off, but one of the nation's major nobles lost his life in the conflict. But apparently that man had been planning a revolt against the current royal family, so most of the citizens took it as some form of divine retribution.

I was amazed that they'd even surfaced in a city like this, though...

From what I understood, the wicked god's aura was drawn to negative human emotions, but maybe they were just becoming indiscriminate in what they attacked.

I also wondered if the Reverse World's boundary was becoming weaker due to the incoming merge... If that was happening, then I needed to figure things out fast. I decided that I needed to hurry up and meet with Elluka immediately, but the girls wanted to take more time with their lunch. That's why I decided to use [Fly] and blast off alone.

Everyone hated going up there with my [Fly] spell anyway, so it was better for me to scout ahead and open a portal for them later. I really wished that they'd just get used to flying, though.

I didn't want to make any kind of undue comment, so I held my tongue and set off, making sure to cast [Invisible] on myself as I rose into the air. I didn't want to get seen by any airships or anything like that.

I ended up going pretty far north, floating above the area equivalent to where the Kingdom of Hannock would be in the regular world.

"She ought to be around here somewhere..." I slowed down, slowly lowering myself closer to the ground as I started scanning the ground below me. According to the map marker, she should've been walking around the road I was nearby.

"Hm… That her?" I saw a figure on the highway in the distance. Two, actually. A wolf-like creature dragging a fallen woman along by the scruff of her neck.

That was absolutely Fenrir and Elluka.

Elluka herself wasn't moving at all, and Fenrir was just dragging her along the road. I wondered if she'd been injured. I dispelled my invisibility and headed over to Fenrir's side.

"Hey, you guys OK?!"

"Hm?! Oh, if it isn't Touya! Are you well?" Fenrir dropped Elluka and turned around to greet me. His voice was as manly and baritone as ever.

"Forget that, what happened to her?!"

"Hm? Ah. Don't fret. My master simply purchased one too many frivolous things in town. She neglected to buy food supplies."

"Seriously?!" I stared blankly for a moment until a loud growl from Elluka's stomach snapped me out of it.

"…Food… Hungryyy…" I pinched the bridge of my nose and heaved a sigh. Was this moron in front of me seriously someone I was hoping could help me defend the Reverse World?

"…Are you okay?" Her stomach growled loudly in response as if to say, "No, I am not okay."

I just shook my head.

"Ahh… That was good! Man, I haven't eaten in like three days or something. Was starting to get worried I'd have to go after bugs or frogs or something gross." I'd pulled a bunch of food, including a few dragon meat skewers, out of my [**Storage**]. The amount she ate could have put Yae to shame… But there was no point worrying about it.

167

"Why are you here anyway, Touya? Don't get me wrong, I'm glad, but still…"

"I was actually looking for you."

"You were? Needed something Gollem-related?"

"Kind of, I guess… I'm not really sure where I should begin but… I guess we can start with you looking at this." I handed her the newspaper I'd picked up earlier and pointed toward the article about the Mutated Construct attack.

Elluka mulled over the words, and Fenrir peeked over to look as well. *The wolf can read, too? That's wild…*

"I see… What about it? I know those golden monsters are a hot topic and all, but what does that have to do with anything?"

"I'll be blunt. Those golden monsters are beings birthed from a wicked god. They can be considered the scouts for an inevitable takeover plan. Soon enough they're going to appear all over this world, and wreak havoc on it. This entire world is in danger, Elluka."

"…Did you hit your head? Do you want me to take you to a doctor?" She looked at me through those thick glasses almost as if she felt sorry for me.

Fenrir was giving me a similar sympathetic kind of look.

Look, I know how stupid that sounded just now, alright?! Gaaah! Fine, I'll give you more details then!!

"Look. My actual identity is the grand duke of Brunhild, I rule over a whole country."

"…You've completely lost your mind."

"…He looks so normal from the outside, this is truly a shame." *Please stop looking at me like that! Auuuugh!* I sighed quietly and shook my head, taking a good few hours to explain the full situation to them. It was far more annoying than it had to be…

"I see, interesting. Well, it's not like what you're saying isn't theoretically possible. This talk of invaders from another world, and a different world in parallel to our own... The whole thing reminds me of Noir's abilities, really."

"Noir?"

"The black crown. It has mastery over time and space. It can pull things through from other realities, but I never expected to meet someone from such a place... Although perhaps it's a little different to how Noir does it. I'm not entirely sure of the chronological specifics..." *Another crown? And this black crown can manipulate space-time? I wonder if Palerius came into contact with that crown five-thousand years back...*

"Either way, you can't expect me to just believe you off the bat. I can hardly just nod my head and accept that you're from another world. That kind of thing is unreasonable. You could be attempting to pull some kind of scam, after all."

"Indeed. If you are trying to trick us with such a story, you must be quite the fool." *Even if I can't blame your skepticism, there's no need to be rude... Then again, I did hardly even manage to convince myself of everything I just said, so it must be even harder for them to believe it.*

The existence of the Phrase would be more than enough to prove what I was saying, but as luck would have it, they hadn't yet attacked this world. Then again, I wondered if that'd count as enough proof after all. Elluka would've probably considered it some new breed of magic beast.

Guess I could just drag her to the regular world and convince her by force...? Oh, I know...!

"I'll show you both something that doesn't exist in this world. That ought to do it."

"Hmm? Something that doesn't exist?" I reached into my [Storage] and pulled out my personal Frame Gear, Reginleif. It landed on the ground with a tremendous thud.

"WHAAAAAAAAAA?!"

"HUHHHHHH?!" If they were cartoons then their eyes would've popped out of their heads. They simply stared on in absolute disbelief at the crystal-lined mech in front of them.

"This here is a Frame Gear. It's a mechanical warrior I created to defend my homeworld from the Phrase, those otherworldly invaders I mentioned."

"A Frame Gear? You mean it's not a Gollem?"

"It isn't. Unlike Gollems, Frame Gears don't act autonomously. They're controlled directly by humans."

"A mechanical frame without a mind? Curious... But yes, that's certainly not like a Gollem. More like a weapon, or a tool."

"Well, we still have sentimental value attached to them. Fighting inside them makes it feel more like a partnership. I think they at least have that in common with the Gollems of this world." I got into Reginleif and made it move around a bit as a demonstration for the two. I got a little too into it and even showed them the Fragarach moves.

I checked through the monitor to see their reactions, and the two of them were about as stunned as I expected. Seemed like this had worked as proof enough that I was something unknown to them.

I hopped out of the cockpit and landed back on the ground, prompting Elluka to charge right toward me.

"Let me have that thing!"

"Absolutely no way." Elluka pouted at first, then started to sniffle, before pulling an expression of such despair that you'd think the world was about to end. I wasn't gonna give up my precious Reginleif that easily.

She threw a little tantrum before finally calming down after Fenrir angrily bit her on the behind. She was still muttering something angry, though.

Since it seemed like they'd been convinced, I shoved Reginleif back into [**Storage**] and began talking to them again.

I basically wanted to know if they had any ways of dealing with the inevitable influx of Mutated Constructs.

"Hmm… Well, this enemy sounds like it can be defeated by strong Gollems, but it might still be a challenge. After all, many of the Gollems in this world lack any combat aptitude at all." That was certainly true. Mr. Sancho's Crab Bus didn't exactly seem useful for anything except transport, it wasn't like it could fight if it had to. The three Etoiles I'd obtained didn't seem all that strong, either.

"Master, would the military-grade Gollems not suffice? They certainly wouldn't lose in terms of sheer numbers."

"Hm… Numbers are one thing, but a bunch of low-quality Gollems won't exactly turn the tide."

"Military-grade Gollems? What are those?" I quickly butted in.

"As a general rule in this world, people typically only own one Gollem. That's mostly because attempting to command multiple Gollems at once causes crossed wires and signal jams… But the military-grade Gollems, or Soldats, don't have any such restriction. A single person can easily command an entire squad of them."

Apparently the Soldats were able to move as a coordinated platoon under the command of individual commanding Gollems known as Sergents.

So a person could take control of a single Sergent, which would then be able to control a platoon of Soldats.

That would prevent any crossed wires since he'd only be commanding one Gollem. That made sense.

"The only issue with that is that all the Soldats are factory models. That means they lack the unique skills that legacy Gollems would have. Not to mention the fact that the amount that can be controlled through the Sergent depends on the individual. I'd say that the average number that can be controlled per person is about five. There's also the fact that all Soldats in a single platoon will be deactivated if that platoon's Sergent is destroyed."

"...So what does that mean?"

"I'll be blunt with you. A single legacy Gollem would probably be better than an entire Soldat platoon."

That was a pain. Ultimately, the situation came down to having a single person control one strong Gollem with a power level of ten, or a single person controlling five weak Gollems with a power level of two. That seemed pretty situationally dependent...

"I have three legacy Gollems under my command, though. I never got anything like that jamming, or crossed wires."

"Three Legacies? Are they perhaps from the same series?"

"Yeah. They're all Etoiles."

"My... That's quite rare. It's almost hard to believe you gathered three Gollems from the same production line, given how many creators there were. It's highly unlikely that there are many others out there with multiple Legacies under their control."

She had a point. The three of them were sold to me because they wouldn't boot up properly. It would make sense that rare legacy models would be snapped up by different people and separated.

"I'd say that if such a situation as you described happens, if this world was attacked en masse... We would have no means of a unified defense." That was bad news. Even if the crowns were powerful, there'd be a limit to how much they could fight. Not to mention the trade-offs for using their power.

The other Legacies would probably be able to handle Lesser Mutants, but Intermediate and Upper Mutated Constructs would be impossible to handle.

But that info wouldn't really help if we had no means of detecting the attack. As far as I knew the Reverse World didn't have an adventurer's network like the Guild, so there'd be no place to reliably install Phrase detectors.

"Actually, Touya... I have a question, or rather, a request."

"Hm? I'm not giving you my Frame Gear."

"Tsk." She seemed annoyed by that.

"While I am personally interested in that thing, let me set it aside a moment. You said you ruled a country in that other world? Something about being a Duke?"

"Grand Duke."

"So you have more of those Frame Gears, right? And you have the authority to relocate them?"

"I have hundreds of them, yeah... They belong to me. Nobody else in the world except my country has them."

That wasn't entirely true, I had given a Dragoon to Ende, but that wasn't relevant.

Ultimately the Frame Gears belonged to me, rather than Brunhild. I didn't use the national treasury to develop them, or anything like that. It was all funded out of my own coffers, usually financed by trade deals with Olba.

"Anyway, I want you to lend the power of those Frame Gears to a small country not far from here."

"What do you mean?"

"That country is currently suffering an invasion, and they're in a spot of trouble. I would like you to help me repel the invaders."

Apparently, the country was a small kingdom known as Primula. They were being invaded by a country called the Triharan Holy Empire. *Let's see here...*

I projected the world map into the air using my smartphone. The map was the inverse of how I usually saw it, but Primula's territory seemed to roughly cover where Xenoahs was in the regular world. Which would make Triharan... This world's territorial equivalent of Yulong.

Guess they're similar here, too... Doesn't matter if it's the regular world or the Reverse World, they're the same kind of people. It reminds me of that time Yulong attacked Hannock.

"What can you tell me about this Holy Empire?"

"It's an extremely authoritarian nation, they have a holy emperor who sits at the top, but he's basically a puppet. The actual political power lies in their senate, and they're the ones who ordered this invasion." Even that sounded similar to Yulong. First an Empire of Heaven, and now a Holy Empire... Geez. Although in Yulong's case, the emperor held all the power alone.

"Triharan is also one of the few nations that makes use of Soldats in its military. In terms of sheer numbers of military-grade Gollems, the Holy Empire only falls behind the Gardio Empire and the Isengard Magitechnocracy."

"Other than those three, there aren't really any other nations that use Soldats."

That just makes it the weakest Soldat-using nation, then! Ah well, I guess it is what it is.

Still, I didn't exactly want to interfere. If you considered every time I'd done that in the past, nothing good usually came of it. Then again, I didn't really need to worry about my social status in the Reverse World.

"I don't really think it's my place to butt in without at least knowing more details. I'd be fine with ending a war, but only if I learn more about it."

"Very well. You can talk to the king of Primula and hear the situation from him, then. There's not much time, though. The battle between the Primula Knight Order and the Holy Empire's army has begun."

Then there was no time to lose. I didn't want more people to die just because I was taking it easy. It didn't matter if it was the Reverse World or not.

"Alright, then let's go quick. [**Levitation**]."

"Wah?!"

"Whoa?!" I took the woman and the wolf floating up into the air with me. Since I was moving anyway, I decided to bring in Yae and the others once I made it to Primula.

"We're about to fly up in the air, alright? Don't move too much. It won't be dangerous, but you might wanna close your eyes. It can be a little scary the first time."

"Flying?! What?!" I didn't give them a chance to protest before casting [**Fly**] and blasting thousands of meters into the air.

It wouldn't take long to reach the destination if I went full-pelt.

My two passengers shrieked in horror as I accelerated toward the Primula Kingdom. For some reason, they were making horrified expressions and looked like they were crying. That's when I realized I hadn't actually made wind-blocking barriers for either of them.

It was a pain to set up on the go, so I just cast [**Prison**] around them and quickly set it to prevent wind pressure from passing through, and maintained an oxygen level similar to that of the ground.

That way I'd be fine to go at my full speed.

Elluka was screaming something at me from inside the [**Prison**], but I paid her no heed.

So long as I maintain my speed, it should only take about five minutes to get there…

Thus, I flew away like a missile, breaking the sound barrier in the process.

◇　◇　◇

"…S-Scary… Too scary…"

"Gwuuuh…" Elluka was looking down at the ground while muttering to herself, while Fenrir was simply flat on the ground, twitching.

Come on, you babies. It wasn't that scary. Just think of it as riding high up in the sky in a supersonic aircraft made out of glass… Actually, that does sound scary. Even though I thought I'd saved time by making it to Primula in just five minutes, they'd been suffering from motion sickness for a full ten.

"…Is this really one of the most renowned Gollem Technologists in the world?"

"I-I am, I assure you…" Hilde, who I had called through a [**Gate**] earlier along with the others, looked over Elluka with a disapproving face. Her doubt was valid, with those thick glasses, tattered clothing, and grumbly disposition, she didn't exactly seem like a genius.

"Oohh… He is so fluffy, he is…"

"Are you really a Gollem? You don't look the part at all."

"M-Miss, I need to inform you that I'm a mighty wolf… Please do not treat me as a house pet…"

"Hm? Are you? Sorry, then." Yae and Elze were frantically petting Fenrir, but let up when he asked them to stop.

I'd introduced my three fiancees to the duo here, but I wanted them to get up and get going already.

"C'mon, we gotta go to the castle. The fight started already, didn't it?"

"Ah... You're right... We need to hurry!" Elluka quickly scrambled up and adjusted the glasses on her face.

Primula's Capital City was known as Primulet, and we weren't too far away from it.

When we arrived at the city limit, Elluka flashed some kind of card to the guards there, and they immediately brought us a six-wheeled Gollem carriage. It seemed like she definitely had connections with the Primula royalty.

We hopped on the Gollem carriage and the knights started taking us along the road to the castle.

I looked out along the streets and saw people with misery cast over their faces. It wasn't surprising, they'd probably just found out they were at war.

The first thing I noticed about the castle up-close was that it was far bigger than the one back in Brunhild. We were greeted by a broad-shouldered, bearded man decked out in fancy clothing. He came charging at us with a smile on his face. He was also extremely fat.

It was honestly comical to see a man of his size running as fast as he could.

"Miss Elluka!"

"Ah, Grand Chamberlain Every."

"What a pleasure to see you, it's been too long!" Grand Chamberlain Every looked to be in his fifties. He stopped for a moment to catch his breath and then shook hands with both Elluka and Fenrir. Although in Fenrir's case it was really more of a pawshake.

"Thank you for coming. His Highness will be so pleased to see you. You'll be able to bring the Primlarge to its fullest potential, no?"

"Elluka... What's the Primlarge?"

"That's this country's royal Gollem. It's a legacy model. I stop by every few years to run maintenance on it." Every turned his eyes to look at me. I had been a bit rude by butting in just there.

"Hm? Who is this?"

"He's an assistant of mine. In fact, if things go to plan, he may be able to repel the Holy Empire's army."

"Wh-Wh-Whaaaat?!" Grand Chamberlain Every's eyes shot open and he sprawled his arms out wide in a ridiculous pose. He would've put a kabuki actor to shame with those moves. He was so ridiculously expressive that I had to hold back my laughter.

"Could you arrange a meeting with the king? Ideally somewhere private... We have a complicated story to tell him."

"Very well! Please wait a moment!" Every wheezed slightly, then patted his chest. After that, he took off running back into the castle. Seeing him totter off like that, I really couldn't help but be reminded of a nursery rhyme character... He was very much a Humpty Dumpty.

As I thought rude things about the chubby old man, Elluka turned and looked into my eyes.

"Touya. Do you know why I believed your story?"

"Hm? Isn't it because I showed you my Frame Gear? And something to do with that black crown you mentioned?" I was curious as to why she'd brought this up all of a sudden.

"Those were factors, true... But there was another reason. This country. You see, of all the nations in the world, this country has the oldest history. Five-thousand-and-two-hundred years ago, there was a world war that ravaged this planet. This country is the

only surviving nation that immediately sprouted up after the war."
I remembered hearing about an ancient world war. If I recalled
correctly, it was started by two major superpowers that enveloped
the world by the end. Something about Gollems running wild and
ruining everything.

The world slowly came back together from the pieces, despite
losing most of its advanced technology... If that was five-thousand-
two-hundred years back, that meant it happened even longer ago
than the Phrase invasion in the world I came from.

"You see, this nation has a legend. They say that five-thousand
or so years ago, in the ashes of the ruined world... A man appeared.
This man spoke a tongue nobody else understood and wielded magic
nobody could comprehend. He was eventually accepted by one
of the small tribes, and with them managed to conquer and unite
the other minor civilizations that sprouted up. He was the founder
of this country. But according to the royal family, he lay on his
deathbed and left us with a series of cryptic dying words. He said
'I am sorry for keeping this from you... But I actually came from
another world.'"

"What?!" Elluka's words shook me.

*The first king of this country was from another world? What the
hell? That can't be...*

"This country is called Primula, after the tribe from that legend.
But the name of the royal bloodline is something else entirely. The
surname of this country's royal family is Palerius. They're all
descended from the first king, a man named Lerios Palerius."

"Palerius?!"

Alerius Palerius... That was the name of the Sage of Hours, a
man who lived in Partheno long ago. He was a master of space-time
manipulation and successfully hid Palerius Island from the world.

But... There's no way he could've used it. Didn't Doctor Babylon say that his gate didn't work...? No, wait... It was that it just didn't have enough magic power.

But... Hold on... If the black crown could pull things from the other world, and maybe visit the other world... Could Palerius have come here? This is too much to take in.

"Is that name familiar to you?"

"...The Palerius part, at least. That's the name of a space-time mage who lived in my world five-thousand years ago. But his forename was Alerius, not Lerios. There's a landmass in the world I'm from named Palerius Island, and the descendants of Alerius live there." If the royal family was really part of the Palerius Bloodline, then that would be interesting...

At the very least it would mean that the people of this kingdom were distantly related to Mentor Central from Palerius Island. But there was still a discrepancy in the timeframe. If this bloodline started two-hundred years before the Phrase invasion in the regular world... Did he somehow travel back in time, or something?

"...Hold on a little... It might be better if I bring someone from that era over..."

"Do you mean Babylon-dono, do you?"

"Yeah. I think she'd be better here. She might have more to add than we would." Elluka seemed confused by my exchange with Yae, so she butted in.

"From that era? What do you mean?"

"Sorry, can you just sit tight a moment? I'll be back very soon."

I left a very confused Elluka behind and teleported myself to Babylon in the regular world with my divinity.

I walked into the Hangar and found several Minibots carrying various tools and attending to their duties. I saw Monica in one of the open garages, she was replacing Gerhilde's shoulder armor.

"Hey, Monica. You seen the doc?"

"Hm? She's like… Right over there, and stuff." Monica pointed in a direction, and that's exactly where Babylon was. She was completely passed out… On the floor, no less… She looked extremely unsightly.

She had a child's body, so this kind of thing would be cute if I didn't know the truth about her. "Ufu… Hehee… You got some good panties, missy… Mind if I see them…? Yeah… Take them off… That's right… Bend over… Ufu… Ahaha…" She was muttering something decidedly un-cute in her sleep. "Wake up, dummy. It's an emergency."

"Huh?" I shook the sleeping, grinning creep by the shoulders to wake her up. She looked at me with half-lidded eyes before reaching out toward me.

"Mm…"

"Gah!" Before I knew it, she grabbed ahold of me and pressed her lips against my face. She'd scuttled up my body and wrapped her arms and legs around me, I was practically immobilized by her grip.

Her tiny tongue probed into my mouth, intertwining with my own as she licked and sucked at me. *Wh-What the hell?! Where did you learn this kind of advanced shit?!*

"Hhghh… S-Stop!"

"Whuh?" I broke her away from me and tossed her to the ground. *That was… Seriously dangerous…*

"Hm…? Where'd my cute little honey go…?"

"You were asleep, you idiot."

Doctor Babylon looked around in a half-asleep daze. Apparently, she'd been dreaming about french-kissing a girl… I set all that crap aside and explained the current situation, then took her to the Reverse World with me.

"Sorry for the wait."

"Huuuuh?!" Elluka and Fenrir weren't too bothered by the fact that I'd suddenly materialized in front of them, but Grand Chamberlain Every almost bent ninety degrees backward and threw out his arms in an exaggerated jazz-hands gesture. Elze had to hold back her laughter at the sight.

"Don't worry, Every. This man can use teleportation magic."

"A-Ah, I see. Forgive me." His breath was a little ragged, but Every managed to compose himself. I felt like if he was born on Earth he'd probably be cut out for making reaction videos.

"Is this child someone from the other world as well, Touya?"

"That's right. She's a doctor named Regina Babylon. She's the creator of the Frame Gears."

"But she's so young!" Elluka stared at her in stunned silence. That wasn't too surprising. At first glance, she just looked like a twerp in an oversized outfit.

Doc Babylon already had [**Translation**] cast on her, so communication would be simple enough. I decided to introduce the two properly.

"Doc, this is Elluka. She's a renowned Gollem Technologist. This is her Gollem companion, Fenrir."

"Most interesting. Oh yes... I quite like the sound of you. I'm Regina Babylon, the pleasure is all mine. I'd quite like to have a discussion with you after all of this."

"I'm Elluka. Actually, I'd like to have a conversation with you, I'm most curious about the technologies of your civilization." The two of them shook hands while attempting to conceal sinister grins on their faces. I wondered what that was all about...

"Hey, Touya... Why are they both making that face? It's creepy..." Elze picked up on it too. I couldn't tell if they saw each other as rivals, and were grinning in a two-faced way... Or perhaps they were happy they'd found a new source of relatively unknown knowledge. Part of me felt like I'd just mixed two elements that should never have interacted.

"A-At any rate, now that we're all gathered... We should head to see the king!" Grand Chamberlain Every, who seemed somewhat shaken by the atmosphere, ushered us toward the castle.

As we walked down the hallway, I stopped to ask Babylon if she'd heard of anyone named Lerios Palerius before.

"Lerios... Yeah, he was old man Palerius' second son, I think. He worked to assist his father, along with his brother. They were pretty into the whole magitech stuff. From what I understand, he died at a young age and his remains weren't recovered." But now I knew the truth. He hadn't died at all. He'd been blown to another world and managed to become royalty there.

As weird as the story was, I actually felt a bit of kinship with the man. My story was basically the same.

We continued through the hallway until we came to a heavy door with two guards standing in front of it.

Grand Chamberlain Every walked up toward the door and had it opened for us. We were checked for weapons, but I had Brunhild in my [Storage], so that was fine.

Yae and the others also had their weapons in the [Storage] pocket of their engagement rings, so they were let through without a word as well.

The door opened into a fairly simple room, but that didn't mean it wasn't pleasant. It looked regal and felt well aged.

There was a man on the opposite side of the room, he stood up from his desk and walked over toward us.

He looked to be in his forties. He was relatively well-built, but was no beefcake. He basically had well-defined muscles along his thin frame.

He had short brown hair and a very neat mustache that flowed into a long beard. He looked like a pretty cool guy. Atop his head was a plain golden crown, nothing fancy.

That meant he must have been the king of Primula. Which in turn made him a descendant of Palerius.

"Good day, Elluka. It has been some time."

"That it has, Your Highness." The two of them greeted each other like old friends and went to shake hands. He wasn't speaking to her like a king would to a commoner.

The king of Primula looked from Elluka toward me.

"And this is the one you said could halt the Holy Empire?"

"That's right. But more importantly, I think he could decipher the stone tablet that the first king left behind. He's from the Otherside."

"He's what?!" After hearing Elluka out, the king of Primula audibly gasped. He looked at me with focused eyes and spoke up.

『Ђтмzт/іоіцо кzттт/аэоці ЂкѓтỸми/іаіоаіі sѕтм/оіэц sѓЂиик/оэааіа?』

"Huh?" I didn't understand what he was saying, and apparently, that made the king annoyed. His eyes narrowed and he was about to open his mouth… But then the same language was suddenly spoken by someone next to me.

"『sѓЂмЂ/оэаао ц』. Is th=at the language that your first king left behind? I'm afraid that there's practically nobody in my world now who speaks Parthenese." Doctor Babylon grinned. *Oh, that makes sense. I could've spoken it if I used my translation spell though…*

Seemed like it was the right call to bring her with me.

"Aha, I see... Is that what you call it? We only know it as the Bygone Tongue, and it is passed down in our royal family. You need to learn it to be able to take the throne, as is tradition."

That was interesting. It was likely that the first king believed that his father would be able to complete the dimensional disruptor and bring the people of Palerius Island to the Reverse World, so he left the language behind...

I couldn't exactly blame him for holding on to that kind of hope. He must have been scared.

He probably thought that the world outside Palerius Island had been obliterated by the Phrase, just like the islanders did.

The king of Primula smiled and took a step forward. He extended his hand to me. He seemed pretty down-to-earth.

"Welcome to my kingdom, friends. Allow me to introduce myself properly, I am King Ludios Primula Palerius."

"I'm the grand duke of the Duchy of Brunhild, Mochizuki Touya. This is Doctor Regina Babylon, and these girls are my fiancees, Elze, Yae, and Hilde." I reached out to shake the man's hand. I couldn't tell if the surprise on the man's face was because of him learning that I was royalty, him hearing the doctor's name, or him realizing just how many fiancees I had.

$$\diamond \quad \diamond \quad \diamond$$

"Take a look at this." I used my smartphone to project a video into the air.

"Oho?!"

"What in the world..." We'd drawn the curtains and closed off the room. The only people in here were me, Elluka, Fenrir, my fiancees, Grand Chamberlain Every, the prime minister, the king, and the knight captain.

I was showing them a recording of a bunch of crystal monsters fighting against massive, mechanical knights.

"These monsters are the Phrase. But the golden ones are mutated offshoots of the species. Right now our world is being invaded by both. For the most part, we've managed to repel them every time they've attacked." I looked around at the people in the room. They were staring in disbelief. But frankly, I didn't care if they believed. I was just here to deliver logic and facts.

"And I know that these monsters have started showing up in your world, too. Eventually, they'll start pouring through in tens of thousands."

"Are you certain about that?"

"Yes. I'm sorry for delivering such blunt news, but the only thing that could possibly fend these things off in this world are legacy Gollems." I felt bad for the people, but I couldn't exactly lie to them. When the two worlds joined as one, this was inevitable.

"...Then if what you say is true... What do you expect us to do, Grand Duke?"

"I want your country to support my efforts in taking these monsters out. I want this country to unify with other countries. In my world, the vast majority of countries have joined together in a league of nations. I'd like to see if the countries in this world could do something similar..."

"You can't expect us to just be at peace with countries like the Holy Empire! They're the same as any other invader!" The knight captain smacked his fist against the table. He was a grizzled looking man in his forties. His red hair was very apt for such a hothead.

"I know it's difficult to reconcile with enemies. That's why we need to reach a state of negotiation first."

"I think if the other side is unwilling to listen, this will be fruitless. It'll escalate to a military conflict no matter what." The abnormally gaunt and thin prime minister chimed in with his opinion. He felt like he'd completely resigned himself to fate. I could understand why he felt the way he did.

"Alright, then. All we have to do is show them a little force, right? Then we can force them to hear us out. How about that?"

"Oho? You mean to crush the Holy Empire, then?"

"No, no. Not that. I don't want to do that, it'd be a major pain in the ass. I'd have to deal with the fallout." I shook my head at Babylon, who was cackling like an idiot. The prime minister was startled by my casual words, but quickly gave me a wry smile.

"It's all well and good to fantasize... But it's not as if you could defeat the Holy Empire."

"Uhh... I mean, I could. If it's just a country, I could go ahead and wipe them out no sweat. What I really hate is the fallout afterward, where I'd have to figure out what to do with the broken nation. I don't really enjoy the idea of conquering nations and expanding territory, honestly." I shrugged slightly, but my words left the Primulan people stunned.

That was just how I felt, though. I was having trouble with Brunhild, and that was a relatively small nation... I didn't want to think about having more territory. I had to be really careful not to accidentally become royalty in the Reverse World. "S-So, Grand Duke... You said you could save us from the Holy Empire, even so?"

"Sure. But the Frame Gears I showed you, those giant knights... They aren't designed to be used against humans, so I won't deploy them."

"Then how do you intend to stop those savages?!" The knight captain yelled again. He and the prime minister weren't exactly treating me with respect. Elze and the others seemed irritated by their behavior, too.

Now that I was having Doctor Babylon talk with them on my behalf, it'd probably be fine, but their attitudes were a little rude for my liking.

To be fair though, I could understand their doubts. I'd just showed up and say "What's up fellas I'm royalty from another world!" As I mulled over such things, the king of Primula reprimanded the knight captain.

He'd gotten a bit mad at the outburst, which was fair. It made a king look bad if his confidants were out of control.

I tried to steer the conversation back on-topic, so I turned to the king.

"Who's in charge of the Holy Empire's invasion?"

"Er... That would be the second heir. Is that right, Prime Minister Beroah?"

"Quite. The second heir to the Holy Throne. Listin La Triharan."

Oh...? An heir? That's perfect.

"Okay. We'll just kidnap him, then. If we can hold him as a hostage, we can just force negotiations."

Everyone except Doctor Babylon and my fiancees opened their mouths in disbelief. They raised their brows and stared at me as if to ask what I was even suggesting. I knew I was saying we should perform a kidnapping, but it didn't seem that bad.

"He can freakin' teleport, people! It would be fairly simple for him to warp into the enemy camp and steal the commander." Doctor Babylon explained it in concise terms. She was pretty much correct.

It was definitely cowardly, but it was simple enough to work well. I didn't exactly want to kill all the invading soldiers... No matter what happened, that imperial commander would end up disgraced, so kidnapping was the path of least bloodshed.

"If... If you could do such a thing, the Holy Empire may well withdraw..."

"Let me just make one thing clear, though. If I kidnap this second heir for you, then our only demand will be a ceasefire. I don't want you taking advantage and asking for ransoms or anything. Obviously, we're not going to hurt or kill the hostage, either." I wanted to end the war, not trash another country. I didn't want them using me for selfish ends.

"And what if they invade again after we return him?"

"I'll just pepper some threats in when I return him. I'll say that next time I'll come for their god-king or something." I had realized at some point that I sounded much like a villain, but there was no going back at this point.

"...You're certainly forceful, Grand Duke."

"I think it's a better tactic than having any more people die. In the world I'm from, countries rarely even have conflicts with each other anymore. Like it or not, this world will have to follow suit as well. Countries that don't co-operate will end up collapsing." I glared softly toward Prime Minister Beroah. To be fair, I didn't exactly mean it. I wasn't about to let any but the most irredeemable of nations fall.

But I also couldn't be everywhere at once. Even if I wanted to save something, I couldn't always manage it.

"Then... Grand Duke. What do you want us to do after all of this, exactly?"

"Once things have settled, I want you to ally with my country. It's not like we have any presence here, though. I'm not really sure how you'd feel about an alliance with a Duchy in another world."

"That's not a problem. I trust you to a degree. My bloodline hails from the Otherside, after all. I don't doubt that such a place exists based on the evidence, and the good words Elluka has for you."

Hmm... To a degree, huh? Guess I still don't have their full trust, but it'll do for now. They might believe I'm a guy from another world, but aren't necessarily convinced I'm a royal.

"Display map. Show the location of the current battle between the Primula army and the Holy Empire's army."

"Understood." My smartphone projected a map of Primula into the air and began to zero in on the location.

Reyvan, huh...? Some kind of fortress city? Seems like the Holy Empire's army is coming in from three directions.

"That seems dangerous, it does."

"Yeah. Seems like they're barely holding the enemy back..." Yae and Hilde muttered to each other upon seeing the situation. It seemed to be a fortified location, but I wasn't sure if it'd last much longer against an onslaught of Soldats.

"Search. Triharan Holy Empire's Second Heir."

"Searching... Twenty-three found."

"That's twenty-two too many..."

"Hrmph..." I grumbled while looking the map over. It meant the search criteria was too broad. Since it was based on my perception, it identified twenty-three people I could mistake for the target. An imprecise spell as ever.

"Do you know anything about what this second heir looks like? Or if you had some kind of image that'd be great. I need to narrow the results."

"Er, well… He's nineteen. He supposedly has a fair and beautiful face. His hair is blonde, too! Ah, and he has a pale complexion due to being sickly. He should also be wearing the Imperial Emblem of his family." *A blonde hunk, huh… Sure would be nice if I was born like that.* I sighed internally as I asked to see what the emblem looked like.

It was two swords crossed together above a two-headed lion. I kept that image in my mind and repeated the search. It provided me with one result.

That meant he must have been the target.

"Alright, I'll be going."

"Oh, take me with you as well." Doctor Babylon suddenly asked to tag along.

"And us, too!" Elze piped up as the other girls nodded.

"Uhh… Sure, I guess?" I definitely didn't want to leave everyone sitting around. Grand Chamberlain Every and the others were obviously still a bit suspicious, so I didn't want them to be left alone.

It'd be better for my own peace of mind if we were together, anyway.

"Alright… The distance is this much… In this direction… I think… [Teleport]." I took my companions with me immediately and teleported off. We landed right in the middle of a tent within the enemy camp.

Since I learned how to use my divinity to travel across worlds, my precision with [Teleport] had gotten considerably better. I could basically do it perfectly within a certain distance from me at this point.

A young man stood in front of us, staring in surprise at our sudden appearance. He seemed to match the description of the second heir, Listin. His hair was a beautiful blond. He basically looked just like the kind of princely man you'd see in manga aimed toward women.

There were also two women in the tent with us, they seemed to be maids.

"Wh-Who are you?!"

"Uhh… I guess we're representatives from Primula? Would you be Listin, Second Heir to the Holy Throne?" The prince immediately drew his sword and pointed it toward me.

"Intruders! Guards!"

"Yikes… [Prison]." I set up a barrier around us within the tent, sealing off the outside.

Soldiers rushed toward the tent with their weapons drawn, but found themselves blocked by an invisible wall within.

"Hiyaah!"

"Oh. Careful, Touya-dono." Listin charged toward me with his sword but Yae reached out and grabbed the blade, twisting it upward and disarming him. It pained me to say it, but my fiancees were clearly becoming something more than human as well.

"Sorry about that, Yae." I grabbed the stunned heir and cast [Paralyze] on him.

As he slumped to the ground, an older-looking knight yelled from outside the tent.

"Bastard! What are you planning to do with our venerable heir?! Return Sir Listin to us at once!"

Oh good, I do have the right person. I'm glad there weren't any mix-ups.

"For the time being, stop your advance into Primula. We'll be keeping ahold of your precious heir until then. I'll return him only when the Triharan Holy Empire is completely out of this country. Understand?! You won't ever see him again if you don't listen to me!"

I yelled my demands out toward the men crowding the tent. The men gnashed and snarled, and directed hateful glances toward me. I kind of wanted them to stop, because I could sense their sorrow... It made me feel like the baddie.

"Truly the words of a villain..."

"That is just how Touya-dono is, it is..."

"...It's certainly not chivalrous, but war forces hard decisions... I shall avert my eyes this once."

"Geez..." *C'mon, guys... This isn't that bad, is it?* For some reason, the doctor was grinning down at the fallen heir, as if she knew something we didn't. I'd cast [**Paralyze**] on him, so he should've still been conscious. He could clearly see and feel Babylon prodding and staring at him.

"Oho... Eheh... Aha... Now I see... Ohhh my... This is most interesting."

She was muttering stuff while patting the guy here and there. Since it was beginning to border on sexual harassment, I dragged her away from him. I didn't want the other side to think we sexually abused hostages...

"Touya. We should bring these maids with us so they can tend to the hostage. We can't just leave it all to Primula, after all."

Babylon spoke up. She had a point.

"You two, please come over here. You can help take care of him while he's in our custody." The two maids nodded and started walking forward. I modified the [**Prison**] to let them pass through, and once they got close they pulled out knives and attempted to stab me in the neck.

I'd expected as much. I calmly dodged their attacks and took them out with [**Paralyze**]. I wasn't an idiot, I knew a battlefield was no place for a regular maid.

"Alright, we'll be taking the heir with us now. If you retreat from Primula, he'll be returned without any harm done to him."

"Do you mean that?"

"I do. I won't let anyone in Primula touch a hair on his head." The man who spoke to me was the same older knight from before, I could sense more intensity behind his feelings than anyone else. I wondered if he knew the heir more closely, perhaps he was a teacher or something. It didn't matter, since I was done with all I needed to do.

I used [Teleport] to move the [Prison] and its contents back to the room in Primula we'd come from.

When we appeared out of nowhere, the Primulan government kicked up a fuss. They weren't startled by me, but rather by the three paralyzed people on the ground.

"G-Grand Duke... Are these..."

"Yeah. The Triharan Holy Empire's Second Heir, and two of his maids." As I explained the situation, I quickly frisked the heir for weapons. I passed his blade, which had the imperial emblem on it, to the king of Primula. That proved it was the genuine article.

I had Doctor Babylon frisk the maids, but she started to massage their breasts halfway through, so I punched her in the head.

"You should be able to hear me. You're in the royal castle of Primula. I'll free you in a moment, so please don't do anything rash. I'll make sure nobody from Primula hurts you." The man nodded his head as much as he could when I spoke to him. Seemed like he understood. I cast [Recovery] on him to undo the paralysis.

He gradually realized he could move his body again, and he stood up. It was only then that I realized just how short he was.

"...You aren't from Primula?" The young man surveyed me with frightened, suspicious eyes. Given that I'd kidnapped him, I could understand his wariness.

"No, I'm not. I'm just a person who wants to end this conflict. That's why I'll fight the Primulan side if they hurt you, too."

"...I feel the same as you. This conflict is pointless. If humiliating me as a hostage is what it will take, then I will accept such a fate."

Huh. Didn't expect that... Seems like he's reasonable. As I pondered to myself, I felt Doctor Babylon tug at my coat. I wondered what she wanted. She very quietly whispered something into my ear. *Wait... Huh?! No way!*

I stared at the man in front of me. What Babylon had told me was true... But the only question was... Why? "What is it, Touya?"

"Nothing..." Elze was curious, so the doctor went and whispered the same thing into her ear. Then, she whispered it to Yae and Hilde. The three of them shot open their eyes in shock. They'd realized the same thing as I.

"Ah... Your Highness. Can you arrange a room for him, please? I'll brief him on the full situation in private."

"Hm? A-Ah... Of course." The king of Primula was still staring at the sword in his hands. He must've still been shocked I'd kidnapped someone so important so easily.

The hostage and his two maids still had [**Prison**] cast around them, so nobody could touch them. Once they were made aware of that, they obediently followed a few knights to their room.

Me, Babylon, and my fiancees also followed them. The Primulan government needed to discuss how to proceed, and I didn't want any part in that... That's what I told them, at least... But I actually wanted to check something else.

I entered the hostage's room and expanded the [**Prison**] to cover the entire area, blocking any sound from leaking out. I didn't want anyone else to hear what I was about to say, after all.

"...I'll introduce myself properly, then. I'm the Grand Duke of Brun... Actually, forget that. I'm Mochizuki Touya. You can just think of me as a wandering mage. This is Elze, Yae, Hilde, and Doctor Babylon."

"A mage?! That explains all the strange things you did... I see."

"Right... So... Nobody can enter this room right now, or hear what we're saying. That's why I need to ask you this... Are you... Not an heir after all? Are you actually... An heiress?" The young man... Or rather, the girl in front of me stopped in her tracks. It confirmed my suspicions. Just as Doctor Babylon had told me... She wasn't a guy!

$$\diamond \quad \diamond \quad \diamond$$

"...How did you know?"

"It wasn't really me, it was the doc here..."

"The shape of your hands and your facial structure are a dead giveaway that you're a girl. Not to mention your body was softer to the touch. Plus I have an excellent ability to sniff out the lewd pheromones emanating from your special spots!" Doctor Babylon... Proudly stated something completely weird and abnormal. She was a degenerate. A goddamn off-the-wall degenerate.

Hilde cast an uneasy glance toward Babylon and then began speaking to Listin.

"Tell me... Are you perhaps a body double for the real heir, then?"

"No. I am the second heir to the holy throne... Listin La Triharan. Though... My real name is Listis Le Triharan." I wondered why she was projecting the image of being male to other nations. That was odd.

Her two maids seemed to be aware of it, which made sense enough. If she didn't want the word getting out, she'd need attendants willing to guard the secret. That was probably why Doctor Babylon asked me to bring them along.

"My father, my mother, and my elder brother are the only others who know I'm a girl... Ah, and Sir Zerorick, my teacher. His wife is also aware... She's named Marr and is the royal physician. Ah, and these two maids are named Lala and Lili." *Her teacher? Guess that Zerorick guy might be the older guy who was yelling earlier.* I tried asking her that, and she confirmed it. While the second heir was formally recognized as the commander behind the invasion, the actual logistics were left to Sir Zerorick. This was Listis' first battle.

"So... What now?" I looked toward the others with a shrug. I thought we were kidnapping a dude, but it was a girl the whole time. I wondered if it would be right to tell the Primulan government.

"I guess nothing changes? Doesn't matter if she's a guy or a girl, right? She's still royalty... So we can still use her as a hostage, right?"

"I'm not so sure..." Listis suddenly cut in on what Elze was saying. I wondered what she meant by that. "The senate probably won't care, even if my father protests. They think of us as mere figureheads, after all. We're disposable when it comes down to it." That sounded bad. I remembered Elluka said something about the senate earlier. "So then..."

"I think in a worst case scenario, they'll just announce that I'm already dead without even trying to negotiate. Then they'll just continue the invasion as scheduled."

I sighed in frustration. I couldn't have expected that kind of outcome.

I realized that they could easily spin it as some kind of holy crusade of vengeance for the death of the people's beloved royalty.

"Mmm… Then… That means there was no point in capturing you, Listis-dono, was there not?"

"I'm afraid that might actually be the case. Or rather, it might have just made things worse. If people start thinking you took me and killed me, it'll only rile up the troops more." *Ah crap… This is bad… If that happens the Primulans are gonna be pissed at me… They'll totally brand me as an idiot who can't be counted on.*

Doctor Babylon looked over at me with a fiendish grin on her face.

"Well then, Touya. What now? Gonna crush the army yourself?"

"You know I can't just do that… Damn it… The only reason I did this was to prevent any further casualties."

"You really kidnapped me for that purpose? You really wanted to put an end to this conflict?" The second heir turned toward me with a hint of wonder in her eyes.

"It's not that I want. It's that I will. It's true that I should've thought about the method a little better… But I thought it would be a lot simpler. This whole war is foolish."

"My father said something similar… But those monsters in the senate still went ahead with their plans. Not even the holy emperor can ignore their decrees, after all… He's just a figurehead for them." Listis spoke in a way that seemed as though she was beating herself up. It sounded like the holy emperor was a reasonable guy.

But I was surprised that the senate had that level of actual control. It was a far cry from the Roman senate I'd read about in history books. I wondered if it was just because it was something in another world, or maybe it had developed differently due to social norms being different… Either way, I understood that this particular senate seemed to be corrupted as all hell.

Apparently, there were about fifty members of the senate, with the senate chairman as the head. The senate was entirely made up of nobility, and it was considered a lifelong position that would be passed on to their children.

It started out as a simple board of advisors until they began to experience a slow creep of power. Eventually, they held authority that exceeded the holy emperor's.

They apparently ignored the pleas of the people and did as they wanted. If anyone ever rose up to try and change their ways, they'd simply crush the voice before it got too loud.

"The current chairman is a man named Morlock Lapitos. He's very old, he's actually close to seventy… But that doesn't stop him from being a force that scares even the other senate members."

"He even scares the holy emperor, though?"

"Officially, the senate is in place to advise my father. That means he cannot propose policies without running them by the senate. That's how they control him. They veto anything that could threaten their authority."

That made sense to me. Groups like that often prioritized themselves over everyone else, even the war they were currently facing was the result of them ignoring the holy emperor.

"But hold on… Can I just ask… Why are you pretending to be a guy?"

"If I were raised as a woman, my father knew that the senate would have forced me to marry one of their children to solidify their political positions. Just thinking about it disgusts me… Originally they planned on saying I was stillborn, but Sir Zerorick volunteered to take me under his wing and train me as a man." It seemed like no matter what world I was in, people were trying to gain political power at any cost…

Apparently, her elder brother had already been made a victim of this. He'd been forced to get engaged to the chairman's daughter.

Apparently, he was completely opposed to the arrangement, because his prospective partner was a lot older than him, and had a hideous personality. I felt terrible for him.

I was glad that all of my fiancees were so kind to me, even if they could get… Scary at times.

"Were you thinking something strange just now?"

"Not at all!"

I answered the very perceptive Elze with a straight face. I wondered when she got so good at figuring me out. Either way, I could understand why the holy emperor and his wife decided to do what they did. I'd also go to any length to protect a precious daughter.

While the crown heir, her older brother, wouldn't be able to reject proposals due to mounting pressures, it would be easier for a secondary heir to reject those things. That didn't mean they didn't care about their firstborn, of course, but their hands were clearly tied.

After all, they hadn't been able to stop him from getting engaged. It was probably a ploy to usurp the throne, anyway. If anything they'd be fine not to marry off the second son, because they'd want his bloodline to die with him.

Ultimately I had gotten the picture. The senate was crooked. They'd gone to all the trouble of orchestrating this war, and then didn't even have any of their families participate.

"So you're saying the best way to end the war would be to do something about that old man and granting the holy emperor's authority back…"

"Y-Yes, that's right! If Chairman Morlock loses his grip, the other senators would be thrown into utter disarray! Father would be able to call back the army, and the Primula invasion would be completely stopped! That's a great idea!" Listis suddenly started yelling and flailing her arms around. I understood her feelings, but she definitely wasn't good at masking her intent. I could see through the fact that she really wanted me to solve the mess.

I decided that I might as well do it, though. That way I'd be able to make some solid connections with the holy empire.

I quickly worked out the pros and cons in my head.

"Alright, how's this then… I take care of the chairman, and you tell your father that the war needs to end. Alright?" I looked straight into Listis' eyes and voiced my suggestion.

She looked shaken for a moment and audibly gulped. Then she began to speak.

"…If you can do it, then I swear upon my very life that I will end this war. Please, mage… Please save Triharan… No, save both Triharan and Primula." I looked over to Elze and the others, and they gave me silent nods.

It was decided. That meant I needed people to help me pull it off. I couldn't exactly take Listis with me due to the political situation and the agreement I'd made with Primula, so I decided that my best bet would be with that older knight. That Sir Zerorick guy would probably be trustworthy. I checked my map and verified that he was still inside the tent I'd kidnapped Listis from.

Alright. I should be able to warp in, grab him, and warp out. Easy!

I was not ignorant of how much like a real kidnapper I sounded at that point. My thoughts were borderline criminal… I was kind of scared by how easily I'd accepted it, it wasn't something I was meant to be proud of!

I decided going alone would be the best course of action this time.

"[Teleport]." I whizzed off to the tent from before and was immediately spotted by several knights. Among them was Sir Zerorick.

They were having some kind of discussion around the central table, probably about figuring out who the criminal was.

"Wh-?!"

"Y-You bastard, it's you!" I dashed through the crowd of knights until I was behind Sir Zerorick. I whipped out Brunhild and pointed the weapon into his back, causing him to sheathe the saber he was holding. He then put his hands up.

"The situation has changed, so he's coming with me too. I'll return him along with the heir, so please don't worry about it. See ya." I said what I wanted before warping me and the new hostage back to the room in Primula castle. I was in and out in under a minute.

"Sir Zero!"

"Oh... Miss!" I let their heartfelt reunion play out for a couple of minutes before briefing Sir Zerorick on the situation. I didn't want him to try attacking me with his sword, so I wanted to clear up the misunderstanding immediately.

After Listis explained the situation, Zerorick went quiet for a while. He folded his arms and closed his eyes.

After a while, he opened his eyes and looked right at me.

"Touya, was it? So I understand you're a mage... Given what I just experienced, I can't exactly refute that. But tell me, what will you do with the chairman? Kill him?"

"No way. Even if someone's wretched, I don't kill. It's not my place to judge him for the foul things he's done, anyway."

"Then what?"

"Hmm... Oh, here's an idea. We could send him and his entire household to an uninhabited island that has no hopes of ever seeing a boat. Or, oh! How about I curse him so he can't speak unless he shoves his fingers right up his nose or something." Everyone except Doctor Babylon drew back from me and gave me a funny look. *Was it something I said?*

I had spells that could suck out people's will to live, spells that could induce sickness, fear, or confusion. Those were just some of the effects of my ancient Dark spells. I was completely equipped with the ability to nullify an opponent without killing them. Hell, I could even rewrite the chairman's memories through [**Hypnosis**] if I really wanted to.

I also had the option of asking the Triharan holy emperor for what he wanted.

I imagined that just searching the chairman's house would end up producing enough evidence of corruption to put him away for life.

"I'd advise caution. He's the chairman, so his entourage of guards is befitting his position. He has several powerful Gollems around him at all times. And it's rumored that he recently managed to hire a personal knight who can use unprecedented abilities."

*He has someone like that? I wonder if he's a spellcaster like me. Or maybe it's something similar to Tsubaki's ninjutsu. Either way, I guess it might not be as easy as I want it to be. But so long as I put my enemy in a [**Prison**] it should be okay.*

"You can leave those Gollems to us, you can."

"Of course, they won't be a problem for us!"

"That's right! I'll crush them all!" My fiancees were excited to fight. But I didn't really want them to overdo it... To be honest the three of them were capable of one-shotting dragons at this point.

"We'll handle the guards and stuff, then. Sir Zerorick, can you explain the situation to the holy emperor?"

"...You wish for me to act as a turncoat within my own nation?"

"If you don't want to, I won't force you... But I'm going to do what I want regardless, so don't complain if you don't help and I end up beating up someone you know." I didn't want him coming up to me and whining that I kicked the crap out of his son or something if I ended up getting charged by random knights. I wanted him to inform the holy emperor so things would be a bit easier.

"Sir Zero, please lend him your aid. If we use his magic, we could maybe even end this wretched senate once and for all..."

"...If the young miss wills it, then I will move these old bones for the sake of ending this foolish war." Sir Zerorick knelt down and bowed to Listis.

... *I'm not asking you to lay down your life, man.*

I used [**Recall**] on Zerorick to get general information about the country and identify the chairman. Then I searched for him using my phone.

I found him pretty easily. He was in the holy empire's capital, in the senate building itself.

The distance was within my [**Teleport**] range. It was approximately as far away as Belfast was from Brunhild, so I was confident I could precisely land there.

"Okay. So first up we'll take out the Gollems and that bodyguard of his, then we'll capture Chairman Morlock and bring him to the holy emperor. After that, we'll see what he decides. Sound good?"

"Sounds good. If such a plan works, that is." I laughed internally a little at her doubt, but I wasn't surprised. I hadn't shown either of them my combat capabilities, after all.

According to the map, Chairman Morlock was on the move. I decided to bide my time a bit and fight when he was in an open space, since fighting in a corridor was a bit of a pain.

Heh... Just gotta wait for the target to move to the center of the main hall, then I'll attack him.

...I'm thinking like a criminal again. Auugh... I'm not a bandit! I'm an honorable grand duke... I am!

He had three knights and five Gollems escorting him. Security was about as tight as I'd expected.

"Sir Zerorick, you should leave the moment we get over there. If you move in and help, things could get complicated."

"...If I must." I activated [**Teleport**] the moment I confirmed with Zerorick that he was in the middle of a large, open room.

We appeared within the room in a matter of moments. In the sudden confusion, Sir Zerorick retreated and hid behind a nearby column.

One of the knights escorting the chairman saw us and yelled out.

"Intruders! Defend the chairman!" Two of the five Gollems answered the call by moving themselves between me and the target.

They were tall and well-proportioned Gollems that looked suitable for combat, and they had knight-like visors down over where their eyes would be. They also had gun-like attachments on their wrists. It seemed like these were the Soldat models I'd heard so much about. One of the five, furthest at the back, looked distinct from the others. It had a horned helmet. That meant it was probably the Sergent, the commander for the Soldat platoon.

"Fire!" The knight yelled out a command, and the two Gollems raised their arms to fire a hail of bullets at me from their wrist-mounted guns. The pace wasn't as rapid as a machine gun, but it was still pretty fast.

"Not so fast!" Elze jumped in front of me, deflecting all the bullets with her gauntlets. I wasn't exactly in a position to say anything, but her abilities seemed absurd...

She had closed the gap between her and one of the Gollems in a matter of seconds, smashing her fist into it and reducing it to a broken pile of scrap metal. She did the same for the second Gollem in just as timely a fashion.

"Do not forget about us, do not!"

"That's right!" Yae and Hilde leaped into action, approaching two of the escort knights and attacking them each. In the blink of an eye, both of the men fell to the ground alongside their armor. They were completely unharmed, but were clearly traumatized by what had just happened.

Their blades were made out of Phrasium, and they could use their inner magic to decide whether or not to slice through the things they were striking. The level of precision that it took to only cut the men's armor off was frankly inhuman... Even I found it absurd.

I felt a little emasculated only watching them do all kinds of amazing things, so I decided to pick up the slack a little as well.

"Come forth, Lightning! Pure Sparking Javelin: [Thunder Spear]!" I scored a direct hit with my Lightning magic on the Sergent unit in the back.

It was completely immobilized as a result, deactivating the remaining Soldats. It was exactly as Elluka had told me. Soldats seemed strong, but that was a pretty crucial weakness.

"Heeey, I wanted to crush them!"

"Ah, sorry." Elze grumbled a bit at me, but I wanted to verify the Sergent's functions.

"Gh... K-Kill them, Weiss!"

"...As you command." The chairman yelled out, and the last remaining knight stepped forward. I couldn't make out his face for his helmet, but he wasn't wasting any of his motions at all. This guy, whoever he was, wasn't some chump. He was probably the knight I'd heard about. I blinked, and he was no longer there. It took me a second to register his speed. I sensed a presence behind me and immediately crouched down low. His sword passed through the space that my head had been occupying not a minute ago. I didn't even notice him get behind me. I stood up and converted Brunhild to Blade Mode and started clashing against his sword. He was good, but he wasn't quite as skilled as Yae.

I was amazed and shocked that I was actually having a hard time against him... So I decided to act without restraint.

"[Slip]!"

"Hgh...!" The knight immediately lost his footing, so I converted Brunhild to Stun Mode and moved in to paralyze him. I felt bad for resorting to something so cheap, but I couldn't have him getting in my way.

That was my plan, at least. But he managed to contort his body as he fell. Brunhild only managed to strike the side of his helmet, knocking it off.

He spun around in the air and attempted to kick me in the side of the head. I managed to dodge the attack and jumped back. I'd underestimated him again. *Alright, if he's gonna be like this then I'll just seal him... With... What...*

"Hey... Hold on... What are you doing here...?" The knight stood up and assumed a combative stance. With his helmet removed, I immediately recognized the face staring at me.

He didn't have the ephemeral vibe that usually accompanied him, but there was no mistaking his identity.

"Ende...?" He showed no reaction at all to my words. I had no idea what he was doing in a place like this. I had no idea why he was acting as my enemy...

I turned to see Elze restraining herself after she saw how I'd almost been hit.

"Hey, Ende! What are you doing here?!"

"…Who are you?"

He coldly answered my words with a glare. I had no idea what was going on…

"It's me, Touya! Mochizuki Touya!"

"Never heard of him." Ende stepped in and slashed at me without hesitating. I stepped back and stared at him in shock. There was no way this guy wasn't Ende, he was powerful enough to actually be a threat. I decided to try casting a little bait. "…Hey, don't you want me to tell you what happened to Melle?"

"…Melle…" Ende's eye twitched, and his body stopped moving. His eyes began swirling around in his head as if trying to find a focus. That meant that somewhere inside him, he remembered the Sovereign, even though he seemed to have completely forgotten me. I wondered if he'd lost his memories… Or if he'd been messed with somehow. "What are you doing, Weiss?! Kill the enemy!" Ende's spasming ended the second the chairman yelled out, and he snapped back into hostility. He came charging toward me with his blade. *Goddammit, this isn't funny! Fine… I'll put you in timeout!*

"[Prison]!"

"Wh?!" Ende was immediately sealed within a pale blue cube. He crashed into the wall of his new container, stumbled backward, and fell to the ground.

He got up and started slashing at the walls, then kicked at the walls, but it didn't give way.

There was nothing he could do. Once you were enclosed in my perfect cell, only something with the power of a god could shatter it.

Hell, it could even hold an Upper Construct if I needed it to.

I decided to leave Ende in there for the time being, since I had pressing questions for the chairman.

"Bastard!"

"Die!" The two other knights, despite their lack of armor, came slashing at me. They were strong, but nothing compared to Ende. But before they did anything, they were unceremoniously stopped in their tracks by Yae and Hilde. *Rest in peace, fellas.*

"You wretches! Do you not know who I am?! I control this senate! I am Morlock Lapitos, chairman of this entire hall! Begone!"

"Yeah, I know who you are. You're an old fart trying to bargain using power that means nothing to me." I spoke frankly toward him, prompting him to snarl and yell. Veins bulged along his red forehead. If he was really pushing seventy, he was doing a good job of hiding it.

He had grey, scraggly hair, and a long beard. He was clad in a fancy gold-embroidered robe. He was also holding an equally fancy scepter in his hands. His body was tall, thin, and gaunt. But his face had distinct traces of arrogance painted all over it. His hooked nose, narrowed eyes, and crooked brow gave off the image of him judging everyone around him.

"Well, I don't really care about you all that much. Tell me what you did to him."

"Him? Ah… You knew Weiss? Heheh…" The old man grinned slightly as he tilted his scepter around in his hands.

"One of my subordinates found that man near the castle, he was quite close to death. He had all kinds of interesting objects on his person… I tried to ask him where he'd obtained them, but it seemed like his memories weren't all there. That's why I had him… Re-educated in one of our special facilities. I renamed him Weiss, and gave him the luxury of serving me directly." *Memory loss… And on the verge of death? That sounds like Sakura's situation… Wait, no. Given that he seems to have been brainwashed, this is way worse. I can probably fix it up with* [Recall]. *Or at least, I hope so.*

But still... Ende, being left on the verge of death like that? How? Who could've been strong enough to do that to him?

"...Heh... And among Weiss' possessions was this! The world's mightiest Gollem!" The chairman pulled a small microscope slide out of his sleeve. *Wait... That's...*

A cracking sound rang out as he broke it between his fingers.

A blinding light enveloped the room, and a massive armored knight appeared, partially demolishing the roof of the room we were in.

It stood tall, sleek, its monotone colors gleaming in the sunlight. I looked it up and down, my eyes settling on its wheels.

It was the Dragoon, the Frame Gear I had given to Ende.

... You seriously let that get stolen, Ende?

"Heheh... You can't even comprehend it, can you?! You're finished!" The chairman scurried up into the Dragoon's cockpit. He moved with such speed and grace that I found it hard to believe he was nearing seventy. The hatch closed around him.

The Frame Gears had been tweaked so even amateurs could control them, even if less proficiently. It was something akin to playing a simulator in an arcade, or a controller on a game console. The Frame Gear itself assisted in some of the processes, too.

But...

"Now, you pesky little worms! Prepare to be crushed beneath my heel!" I ignored the voice of the old man that was blaring through the Dragoon's speakers, and I pulled out my smartphone. Then I pushed a button.

"Ahahahaaaaa, huh?! Wh... Huh? Why isn't it moving? It moved fine before...?!" The voice coming from the speakers descended into panic. The Dragoon slowly lowered itself, and showed no signs of getting back up.

Yae let out a sigh as she looked up at it, while Elze just grinned and shrugged her shoulders.

"He is truly a fool, he is."

"Well, it's not like he could've known, right?"

"Move! Gah! Move, damn you!" As he continued to freak out, I hopped up to the cockpit and unlocked the hatch that was protecting the manual open/close lever. I pulled it.

With the hissing sound of whooshing air, the cockpit sprang open.

"Eek!"

"Sorry to burst your bubble, pal... But I invented this thing. That makes me the master of this Gollem. Understand?" ...*Technically, this was invented by Doc Babylon, Rosetta, and the others... But I'm not gonna sweat the small stuff.*

There was an emergency override built into all the Frame Gears. Given how powerful they were, that was a perfectly normal safeguard.

"W-Woaaah!" I used [**Levitation**] to forcibly remove chairman Morlock from the cockpit. He flailed his arms and legs in an attempt to resist, but it was futile. When I brought him back down to the ground, Zerorick came back out of hiding.

"Oh! Z-Zerorick! Strike this fool down! He's trying to destroy our holy empire!"

"I'm afraid not."

"Wh-What?!"

"This man has Lord Listin as a hostage, you know? I'm afraid my hands are tied, Chairman. I can't do a thing." He attempted to hold back a grin as he said that. I was amazed by how smooth this guy was, he actually used the hostage situation as justification.

"Y-You idiot! What do you think is more important?! Me, the vital and important chairman, or Listin, an incompetent second-born?! I'll have you executed for this!"

"Enough."

"Grugh?!" Elze, clearly fed up with his rambling, chopped him hard in the back of the neck. I was getting tired of him too.

I wondered how he had the gall to say something like that. This country had a lot of problems if it was letting a man like this sit at the tippy-top.

I gave Sir Zerorick a reassuring pat on the back, but the moment of sympathy was held up by a cracking sound. I turned around to see Ende physically breaking out of the [**Prison**].

"What the hell?!"

No way... I know I didn't pour divinity into it this time but normal attacks can't possibly break through it! Ende had two blades in his hands that I hadn't noticed. They weren't quite long enough to be considered longswords. *Wait... What's that coming off them...? What... How?*

I dodged the strikes from his blades by jumping back, then quickly chanted a spell.

"Spark forth, Ice! Frozen, Jolting Maelstrom: [Vortex Mist]!"

"Hrgh!" Ende got his hand caught in the sudden mist cloud, shocking him enough that he let go of one of his weapons. I reached in and grabbed it, then jumped back. I took a closer look... And it was exactly as I'd suspected.

The shortsword in my hand had divinity leaking from it. There was no mistaking it... He was wielding a Sacred Treasure... A weapon bestowed by the gods.

"How did you get something like this, Ende..." Sacred Treasures were gifted to worlds as a last-hope kind of deal when they were threatened by wicked threats of divine origin. Heroes usually wielded them to repel the enemy, and the items were commemorated in legend and myth.

Since Sacred Treasures could become potential birthing spots for wicked gods if they weren't handled properly, they were usually destroyed or replaced with a replica after their purpose was served. That's what I was told, at least.

"Haaah!" He charged forward with the remaining blade in his left hand.

Guh... This is getting annoying, Ende! Get your shit together!

"[Accel Boost]!" I charged headlong toward Ende.

"Wh-?!"

"Don't take this personally... But Yumina asked me to hit you for her." I smacked Ende right across the face and sank my free fist into his stomach.

"Bwugh!"

"Go to sleep." After he keeled over, I brought the hand I'd used to slap him down over his neck in a chop. The remaining Sacred Treasure fell from his hand, and he collapsed on the spot.

"He was certainly going all-out, he was..."

"Indeed. He almost gave you a run for your money, Touya."

I was mostly just annoyed at Ende. Sure he'd lost his memories, but I wasn't so keen on him acting like this.

I picked up both Sacred Treasures and threw them into [Storage], then sealed Ende in another [Prison]. I decided to wait a bit before recovering his memories, I had other fish to fry.

I shrunk down his holding cell until it was the size of a die, and slipped it into my pocket.

Unlike [Storage], time wasn't halted within the enclosed space... I decided to hurry up and finish things before the guy woke up and needed to use the bathroom.

I cast another [**Prison**] around the chairman, and Zerorick took me toward the holy emperor. I took that opportunity to recover the Dragoon as well.

The whole stuff with the Frame Gear raised a commotion, so several soldiers were in the area. I ended up using [**Invisible**] to mask us, so we got by without any hassle. According to Zerorick, entering the palace was usually forbidden unless the Senate expressly permitted it.

Given that this was the home of the holy emperor, I expected the palace to be a little gaudier... It honestly looked plain compared to the grand senate house we were in earlier.

There weren't many Gollems or knights on guard duty, either. It really put into perspective that the holy emperor didn't mean much in this country.

"Your Highness!" Sir Zerorick opened a door at the end of one of the hallways and yelled out. There was a man in the room sitting at his desk with a book. He seemed to be in his fifties. When he heard the voice, he looked around in confusion.

The man had white hair and a small white beard, as well as a pair of round glasses on his face. He looked much like an academic. Not the image I expected of the Triharan holy emperor. There was nothing intimidating about him, really... But that wasn't too bad, he seemed fairly casual.

I quickly realized why he was looking around in confusion. I'd forgotten to cancel our invisibility spell.

When I finally undid it, the shock of our sudden appearance made the man fall out of his chair.

"Uwah! S-Sir Zerorick?! A-Are you not supposed to be on the Primulan front...?"

"Please forgive me, Your Highness, but I am here to ask something urgent of you. It's a matter that could decide the fate of our holy empire." The holy emperor looked confused, so Zerorick pulled out a letter from Listis explaining the situation, and handed it to him.

At first, he seemed skeptical and confused, but then I pulled open the [**Prison**] I'd used to contain Chairman Morlock and sent the older man tumbling to the ground.

"...I see... This is serious indeed. Guards! Bring Lupheus to me at once!" A guard peeked his head in from the outside, then nodded and ran down the hall.

I asked Zerorick something that I wanted to be sure of.

"Who's Lupheus?"

"The firstborn son, crown heir to the holy throne." That made him Listis' older brother. Given how poorly the holy emperor was treated, I wondered how badly he had it in daily life.

After a while, the knight from before brought a young man into the room.

He had golden blond hair just like Listis. He was definitely in his early twenties. He was fairly handsome, and the glasses he wore gave him an intelligent aura like his father's. He didn't seem the type to take up a blade and fight on the front.

When he entered the room, he was initially shocked and confused, but after his father and Sir Zerorick filled him in on the details, a fire seemed to light up in his eyes.

"Father! This is a golden opportunity! This is a chance for us to abolish that dreaded senate and restore peace to our entire empire! If we listen to this man and end the war with Primula, we can work toward peace!"

"Hm... Mm... Yes... You're quite right." His speech was so loud and passionate that he even seemed to unnerve his father.

I remembered that he'd been forced to get engaged to the chairman's wretched daughter… I'd heard she was a lot older and had a crappy personality, so he was probably desperate to get out.

I asked about it later and discovered she was in her forties, had a sadistic streak, and was so hideous a lot of people mistook her for a guy. I could understand Lupheus' desperation.

The senate held absolute power, but it wasn't integral to the country's government. If it was abolished, there'd be some initial confusion, but things would eventually settle.

The senate had treated the holy emperor and his family as disposable, only to be disposed of by them in the end… A cautionary tale indeed.

"Very well. Lupheus, take some guards and some Gollems, search the estate of the chairman's family. I am certain that evidence of his embezzling will be in there somewhere. Zerorick, head out and order a retreat of our army. We shall make peace with Primula this day."

"And what do I do with this guy?"

I pointed toward the chairman, who was still flat-out unconscious.

"…This might not be fitting with due process, but… We'll have him imprisoned in the dungeon until we find evidence of his guilt." Normally you wouldn't go locking someone up without proof, and hearing that statement without context would make it seem suspicious… But there was no doubt that he was guilty of what he had done.

I was sure that the other members of the senate wouldn't be let off too lightly, either… But in the end, what goes around comes around.

Lupheus made off for the chairman's estate immediately. He definitely seemed happy, not that I could blame him.

I asked the holy emperor for a handwritten letter that I could pass on to the king of Primula, then took Zerorick and my fiancees to the camp we'd initially kidnapped him from.

He immediately gave the order to retreat, but was met with slight resistance by some nobles who were visiting. Apparently, they had ordered some men to pillage spoils of war from the conquered city.

The moment we showed them the emperor's letter and told them the senate was to be dissolved, they quieted down really quickly.

Seemed like they'd been plotting bad stuff in the background, too. Seeing that their senate-based backing would soon be over likely sent them into a panic. It was too late for them, either way. Sir Zerorick wouldn't miss their guilt.

After the order to retreat had been given, I warped us back to Primula castle.

I passed on the letter from the holy emperor to the king of Primula and told him the war was officially over. Everyone simply stopped what they were doing and stared at me blankly.

I couldn't blame them, to be honest. It had only been six hours since Elluka brought me to the country. The fact that I'd saved not one, but two nations from disaster, was not something any reasonable person should have to understand.

"How can we even begin to express our gratitude?"

"Nah, seriously… It's fine. I could only come to this world to begin with thanks to the device your ancestor made, so really I should be thanking you."

Everything was just about done, so we headed over to see Listis. When she saw me, Zerorick, and the king of Primula, she heaved a sigh of relief.

Sir Zerorick summed up what had happened while we were away.

"Amazing! I can't believe it."

"Indeed. The senate is dissolved and the chairman is imprisoned... This is a bold new future for our holy empire!" Zerorick and Listis grinned happily toward each other. I was glad that she was now free from living a life of pretending to be someone she wasn't.

Elze and the others were smiling too.

"I'm glad the war's over."

"Same here. It happened faster than I expected."

"All is well that ends well, it is."

Though everyone was happy, I was still pretty bummed out. Because even though the mess in Primula had been resolved...

"I've still got another mess to deal with..." I sighed softly as I looked down at the die-sized [**Prison**] I'd just taken out of my pocket. Ende was still out cold inside it.

$$\diamond \quad \diamond \quad \diamond$$

The two nations signed a peace treaty, and the war finally came to a concrete end.

Everything from then on was up to the two countries, I wasn't planning to interfere any more than I had. Well, I did safely return Listis to her family.

Though there was some slight resistance, the holy empire dissolved its senate, and most of the senators were imprisoned and had their estates repossessed.

The chairman and the corrupt senators would likely receive their sentences, but I didn't care enough to find out their fates.

I'd also managed to secure connections and support within the Reverse World's governments; two nations now trusted me.

I hadn't exactly created a sturdy defense against the inevitable Phrase attacks, but it was a start.

Just as I was about to call it a day and head home to Brunhild, another problem came up.

"Take me with you!"

"Uhh…" Elluka started whining that she wanted to come with me. *Please stop clinging to my leg like that… Elze and the others are staring daggers into my skull right now!*

"Touya, she definitely has a lot of good know-how. There's stuff I wanna ask her about, too… So let her tag along."

"Thanks, Regina! I knew you were reliable!" Elluka winked and pointed toward Doc Babylon. Even though I knew she was intelligent… Her personality was a pain. I wasn't sure if I wanted her and Babylon talking unsupervised.

Fenrir coming along too was a little bit of a relief, but I wasn't sure if it was completely reassuring.

"When you say let her tag along, you mean take her to Babylon?"

"Yeah. We won't have her roaming around the ground, so we'll just let her hang around the workshop or the research laboratory." *Hmm… If her Gollem research can help us improve the Frame Gears, then it might be indispensable for the coming conflicts…*

I looked over toward Elze and the others. They all nodded.

"Why not, right? She's probably gonna be helpful."

"Well… If everyone says so, then…"

"Wahoo! We did it, Fenrir! We're going to another world!"

"I'm glad for you, master." I felt a teeny bit anxious as Elluka immediately lifted up Fenrir by the front paws and started dancing with him.

"Another world, eh… Touya, please take me there someday. I'd like to see the world of my ancestors."

"Someday, for sure. I'll introduce you to another person on that side from the Palerius lineage, as well. She's quite pretty, you know."

"Ohoho, I like the sound of that." The king of Primula laughed and shook my hand. I promised I'd return, and told them that if anything dangerous happened, to look for the Silver Dragon on Drakliff island.

I ordered the dragons on that island not to harm any humans unless they attack first. Most of them didn't speak the language of humans, but they pretty much all understood it. So long as they explained what they were there for, Shirogane would be able to help them out.

"See you later, then."

"Mm. Thank you again for helping us. Farewell." I waved off the king of Primula and used **[Gate]** to take us all back to Drakliff island. Then we used the Dimensional Disruptor Mk. II to return to Babylon.

I asked Elluka to wait a little bit because I wanted to fetch Yumina. I didn't exactly suspect Elluka of anything, but I wanted Yumina's Mystic Eyes to determine her intentions.

Yumina judged her to be pure of heart, so I had Doctor Babylon give her a tour of the place. Elluka was already looking around in a mixture of confusion, awe, and wonder.

They were getting pretty hungry, so I warped Elze and the others back down to the surface. Just as I was about to warp the two of us back down, Yumina tugged at my sleeve.

"Touya… That woman isn't going to be a tenth, is she…?"

"Absolutely not! Hell no! She's just another member of staff, I promise!"

"Alright, then." Yumina was smiling, but I felt a frightening amount of pressure behind that face of hers. I hoped she understood I had no plans to increase my wife count.

I didn't understand why she was fine with me having mistresses if she got that concerned about more wives... Not that I was planning on having any, anyway.

Yumina and the others seemed to consider Doctor Babylon and the Babylon Gynoids as my mistresses already, apparently. I wondered if they were fine with me having mistresses so long as they were infertile or something.

"Oh, right. I met Ende in the other world. That dumbass had lost his memories and gotten brainwashed."

"Wow, really? What happened to him?"

"Hm? Oh, I beat him and put him in this cube." I pulled out the die-like [Prison] and tossed it out on to the grassy knoll in front of us.

"Release." Registering my keyword, the [Prison] shattered apart and released its prisoner.

In a matter of seconds, Ende charged at us. He was dashing toward Yumina with his fist about to fly right at her.

"Gaah!"

"Eek!" *Goddammit!* I caught his hand just before it struck Yumina, then tossed him over with a perfect ippon seoi nage judo throw. When the dumbass was flat on his back, I hit him with [Paralyze].

"Gwaugh!" After he went limp, I let go of him.

"Sorry... Didn't realize he'd woken up yet. That's one drawback of [Prison]." Time flowed normally in there, unlike [Storage], so he'd probably woken up a while ago. He'd been biding his time and waiting for his opportunity.

I was pretty livid that he'd tried to hit Yumina of all people. I wanted to hit him a few more times.

"He's certainly out of his mind, then…"

"Yeah… His memories are probably all jumbled up. I'm gonna bring him to Melle and hope he can come back to his senses." It'd be bad if he kept attacking us no matter what.

I lifted his body up with [Levitation] and made for Babylon's rampart with Yumina.

We reached Melle's room, and I set down Ende on the ground near the despondent girl.

"Endymion?!" Melle, who had been unresponsive since I left her, suddenly snapped to her senses and began cradling the unconscious man in her arms.

"This is awful… Who did this to you?"

"Ah… That was me, kinda… But hold on! Don't get upset! I'm sorry! It's not my fault! He lost his memories and tried to attack me…! It was self-defense, okay?! It was just self-defense!" Melle looked up at me with teary eyes, sniffling softly, so I spewed out my defense. I ended up getting a little excessive, but I didn't really like being guilted.

"His memories?"

"He was apparently on the verge of death when he was found. He lost his memories as a result, and after that, some bad guy implanted bad ideas into his head, which made him see me as an enemy. He seemed to remember you a bit, though."

"…I understand. I'll heal his mind at once."

"Huh?" Melle completely ignored me and extended her fingers until they took the form of thin, crystal tentacles. They snaked outward and latched on to various parts of Ende's head.

"I'll undo the psychological damage that Endymion has suffered. You may wish to cover your ears, the sound is rather shrill."

The moment she finished speaking, the tendrils began emitting a piercing shriek. It rippled through the air, causing an amplified tinnitus-like sensation. I couldn't stand it, so I backed out of the [Prison] with Yumina.

"Did she say this was healing him?"

"It might be similar to my [Recall] spell, or maybe she's using vibrations to mess with his brain." I could only really guess, but being in there made me feel like I was in a microwave oven. I hoped Ende's head wouldn't explode or something.

After a while, Melle turned toward us and made a puzzled expression. Something seemed to be wrong. Yumina and I stepped back into the [Prison], Melle began speaking in a concerned manner.

"Umm… I should have fixed him, but he's not moving…" Ende's eyes clearly had life in them. He was laying atop Melle's knees, but he couldn't move or talk. He moved his eyes to shoot me a glare.

"Oh, right… I used [Paralyze]." I'd totally forgotten, it was no wonder he couldn't move.

I walked up to Ende and cast [Recovery] on him. I decided that I'd cast [Paralyze] on him again if he tried anything funny, though.

After I undid his paralysis, Ende reached a hand out to Melle's face, and gently caressed her cheek.

"Hey, Melle. Been a while, huh…"

"Endymion!" Melle held him tight against her.

It seemed like he was back to his old self. I was glad.

"You have your memories back…"

"Thanks to you… I remember what happened when I lost my memories, as well… Touya, you hit me pretty hard."

"That's all your fault, man. Can't blame me for it." If he could speak to me so casually, that meant he was fine. Ende looked around the room with narrow eyes as Melle embraced him.

"Touya... Why is she in a place like this? Did you bring her here by force?"

"...Please don't make me out to be some kind of kidnapper. This is for her own protection. The Phrase can't sense her while she's in here. This space is completely isolated, so it's the safest place in the world for you both." *Don't make me out to be some kind of kidnapper.* I was pretty angry that Ende was assuming I'd do something like that, so I met him with a light scowl.

We continued to stare each other down until Yumina stood between us.

"Let's allow Ende and Melle some time to talk their personal business out, okay? We'll take our leave for now."

"Huh? Wha- Yumina?!" Despite my protests, Yumina dragged me right out of the [Prison] and into the corridor. I wondered what that was all about. "That's enough, Touya. The two of them are lovers, aren't they? They've been separated for a long time. You can't sour their reunion with a petty argument. There's no wonder he'd be suspicious if he found her confined."

"...Ah... I mean, I guess." Yumina explained the situation, and I looked back at the door with mixed feelings. *Guess I was a little dense... My bad...*

At least I knew now.

"...As they say, he who interferes with love needs to get kicked by a horse and die."

"Do they say that?"

"Back in my birth country, at least. The idea is that infringing on people's romance is such a heavy-handed thing to do that getting kicked in the head by a horse is the only suitable punishment." Well, it wasn't like I meant it literally. If I got kicked by a horse I wouldn't die with the body I had. There was a lot I wanted to ask of Ende, but I decided to respect him for the time being, along with Yumina's wishes.

Besides, it wasn't like he could escape the **[Prison],** and I'd taken his Sacred Treasures, as well.

The two of us walked away from Ende and Melle's room.

"Alright, time to hear you out." I rapped my knuckles against the table Ende and I were seated at. We were in a dim room, only illuminated by a dim amount of Light magic, but it was enough to see his face.

"Let's make this real easy-like... I wanna hear the whole story. Want a cutlet? Reminds you of your mother, right?"

"...Touya, you're acting pretty weird... But I am hungry, so I'll have some." ... *Guess I got a little carried away there... Usually, in interrogation scenes in TV dramas they offer culprits some katsudon, but I guess it's not the same here...*

Cesca brought in three bowls of pork katsudon. One for me, one for Ende, and one for Melle... If she actually ate.

"Is that for me?"

"I know the Phrase don't need to eat or whatever, but it's been cooked so... You might as well try it." Melle turned to Ende, she seemed puzzled. But once she saw him pick up his chopsticks and eat the cutlet, she awkwardly followed suit and put a bite into her own mouth.

"Oh?!"

Melle's eyes went wide and she began happily chowing down. She seemed to really like it.

"...What's the relationship between Dominant Constructs and food, anyway?"

"The Phrase, in general, can operate just fine so long as there's a little sunlight and magic power, so they're not really versed in the many flavors out there. Although, Lycee was pretty big on food."

"I see... Actually, what happened to her? Wasn't she with you?"

"I'll get to that later. Let's enjoy our food, first." That was fair. I wanted to finish my bowl before it got cold, after all. It was delicious... Which probably meant Crea had made it. Then again, it could've also been Lu. Even though she was a princess, she was on the level of a pro chef when it came to kitchen antics.

We finished our food, even though Melle seemed like she wanted more, and Ende began to speak.

"You know about them, right? Those golden Phrase, I mean."

"The Mutated Constructs?"

"Mutants, huh? Yeah, that's a good term for it. The Phrase that came to this world have divided into two factions. There's Ney's group of loyalists and Yula's group of insurgents. Yula got some weird new power from somewhere, and is capable of morphing the species into a weird hybrid species." *I think I remember meeting Ney one time... And Yula's probably that other guy who creeped me out. I remember thinking his eyes were shady, so he must be the guy with the wicked god's power.*

"I was attempting to figure out the power of Yula's faction, and I tracked them down in the gap between worlds. It was there that I met with the twins, uh... They're two Dominant Constructs named Leto and Luto. They defeated me. It's a little embarrassing to admit, honestly... But they completely overpowered me. They were far stronger than they'd used to be, it came as quite a shock. They'd been infected with that golden stuff, and their power had increased along with that change. It took everything in me just to get out of there."

"…They've got more Dominants on their side? And you're telling me some of them are mutated already?"

"That power of theirs is not of this world. I've traveled through many worlds before, Touya… What I'm about to say might shock you. They have… The power of a god. They have unthinkable might, a power that could create or destroy worlds!"

"Nah, not quite. They actually have a wicked god's power. It's more of an imitation god that was born in the mortal realm, the power they're currently wielding is nothing compared to actual divinity." Ende stared at me with a blank face. He blinked. It was clear from his vacant expression that he had no idea how I could know this. I ended up snickering a bit at how dumbfounded he'd become.

"…There's been something on my mind for a while, Touya. Just who are you, exactly? It's clear you aren't an ordinary human."

"Ah, well… I guess it's fine to show you two." I cleared my throat and triggered my Apotheosis, letting divinity flow through my body and seep out into the room. I let out just enough for the two of them to notice.

When the wave hit them, they both opened their eyes in shock and backed away a bit. *Might've overdone it a little…* I changed back into a regular human and nodded toward them.

"That… aura just now…"

"Yeah. Basically, I'm a god. A trainee one, but… Yeah."

Ende and Melle stared with their mouths hanging open. I couldn't exactly blame them for it. The aura granted by my

Apotheosis basically forced anyone bearing witness to it to acknowledge me as a god on some fundamental level. Mine wasn't quite as powerful as Karen and the others' yet, though.

"…Sh-Should we be praying to you?"

"Please don't, that'd just be awkward. I'm a god-in-training, not a fully-fledged one yet. So please just treat me normal." The two of them glanced at each other and leaned forward a bit. They still seemed a little uncomfortable, but I was sure they'd get used to it.

"So… You lost your memories after the twins beat you up?"

"…You don't have to say they beat me up… I mean, they did… But still… Either way, no. I managed to escape. The issue came when I realized what I was up against, so I set out to obtain a power to rival theirs."

"Are you referring to these?" I opened up my [Storage] and pulled out the two shortswords. They were Sacred Treasures.

"That's right. They're weapons from a world a few steps away from this one. The world was under attack from some evil dragon something or other, but it was saved by a hero who wielded these blades. The swords were passed down that hero's family line or whatever, so I decided to borrow them." *You nabbed some Sacred Treasures from another world?! Well… I guess having them lying around could've been dangerous, so Ende having them is fine.*

"But then a mysterious man appeared in front of me. He said 'Whoops, we forgot to retrieve these, can't have these lying around the mortal realm,' and beat the crap out of me when I refused to hand them over. I used my ability to jump to another world just before I lost consciousness, but I ended up landing in the wrong world. After that, the old man picked me up and the rest is history."

Retrieve…? Lying around the mortal realm? Was that a god, maybe? I asked the two of them to excuse me for a moment, then made a quick call to God Almighty. I explained to him the gist of the situation, and he merrily replied.

"Ooh, that was the god of battle! He has been talking about that encounter, he said he would like to take on that young man as his apprentice since he is so very promising. Ah, also... You may keep the swords. Just make sure not to lose them, please!"

Well. That answers that.

It was honestly pretty amazing Ende had survived against a god like that... But at the same time, he almost died and lost his memories as well. So it was just barely surviving.

I told Ende who he'd faced up against, and he smiled wryly.

I could understand his feelings. He'd gotten his ass beat by the twins, gotten his ass beat by the god of battle, and then gotten his ass beat by me. It was three major losses in a row. I felt sorry for him; it wasn't as if he was weak or anything.

I put the Sacred Treasures back into my [Storage] for the time being.

"Well... Now I know what happened to you. But what about Lycee?"

"I sent her to Ney. I asked her to explain a few things, like the mutants and so on... They are sisters, you know." I didn't know that. They hardly looked alike.

I wondered how family relationships even worked with the Phrase. Hell, I didn't even know how they reproduced. I decided it wasn't the time to ask about that, so I left it be.

"So what are you planning on doing with us, Touya?"

"Well... As crummy as it is, I can't let Melle out of here. Not for the time being, at least. I don't want the Phrase launching a full invasion against my country. And as for you, Ende..."

He wasn't exactly our ally in this situation, he was more on Melle's side. The situation was stickier than I'd have liked.

"I'll work with you, Touya, so long as you guarantee Melle's safety. Now that we've come this far, we might as well put an end to this madness once and for all."

"I… I wish to speak with Ney and Yula. I would like to face them head-on… And tell them to put an end to this. I know it may be difficult, but still…" Melle looked down at her hands as she spoke. Before we could do that, we needed to wait and hear back from Lycee. Still, it was unusual that neither Ney nor Yula had made a visible move in a while.

"So for now we'll live our day-to-day lives until something new comes up. You'll both be in my care until then."

"Whaaat, me too?!"

"You'll keep her company as punishment for letting her be alone for so long. Don't worry, we won't check on you all that often, so feel free to get handsy."

"Wh-huh?!" I grinned and turned to leave the room. Ende was flustered, and Melle was glowing red in the cheeks. Before I left, I noticed that Ende and Melle were holding hands under the table. I had a feeling that Ende being there would do a lot of good for the poor girl's mental health.

"Have the talks finished, have they?" I headed into the rampart's living room, and Yae greeted me. There were many empty bowls filled with crumbs on the table. I wondered just how many cutlets she'd eaten…

"Yeah, pretty much. If things go well, we won't have to fight the Phrase again. We'll probably have to fight the mutants, though."

"That is excellent news, it is. Oh, also, a letter came from my elder brother, it did. He says he wishes to have a rematch with

Moroha, he does. He wishes to know when a good time would be." *A rematch? Huh? When did those two ever fight?* "It was during the martial arts tournament, it was. My brother won, he did. So Moroha fought against him afterward, she did." *Ahh… Back then. That was the last day of the festival, so I was out cold because of the fight with Gila.*

I asked more about it and obviously, Moroha won without any difficulty. That came as no surprise to me. From what I was told, she also went all-out against the hapless bastard. She was more of a demon than a god, really.

"I feel kinda sorry for the guy, but I'm pretty sure he'll just lose if he tries again…"

"He himself believes that as well, he does. But he wishes to use the opportunity to train."

If it was just that, then it'd be fine. I was glad he seemed to be a pretty upbeat guy. I'd have felt guilty for bringing Moroha down here if she ended up crushing his resolve.

My smartphone started ringing, so I pulled it out of my pocket. It was a call from Kousaka. For some reason, I had a bad feeling…

"Yeah, 'sup?"

"Your Highness. I would like for you to get through all of your work for the day, else there may be complications down the line. Where are you?"

"Ah, right… I'll be right there…" The recent issues in the Reverse World had been distracting me, so I had a lot of affairs to catch up on in relation to Brunhild.

Ultimately my work as grand duke mostly came down to approving or denying planning proposals. Guildmaster Relisha had recently agreed to build a school for adventurers, so I needed to get on looking at that.

Apparently, a lot of newbies had come to Brunhild because of our dungeon islands. That meant there were a lot of cases where untrained or inexperienced adventurers were pushing themselves to the point of injury or even death. A school would help teach the skills to prevent such tragedies.

There was no downside to enrolling in a school that could teach you how to stay alive, that's why I wanted to keep enrollment fees down as well.

I decided to do my job and go help out Kousaka.

"I'll go take care of work for now. Later, Yae."

"Be safe, Touya-dono." Yae waved me off as I opened a **[Gate]** to Brunhild castle.

◇　◇　◇

Leen was riding in Grimgerde. The massive Frame Gear raised its right arm and began firing its Gatling gun.

Hilde's Siegrune lifted its shield and deflected the attacks. She attempted to charge forward, but a grenade detonated at her Frame Gear's feet, causing it to stumble.

"Hold out a bit longer, Hilde!" Lu's Waltraute stood atop a nearby hill, taking aim with its shoulder-mounted cannon. Its target was Leen's Grimgerde.

It was currently equipped with the C-Unit, meant for long-range shots. Its heels had it anchored into the ground. A mighty roar echoed through the air as a huge bullet came out of the barrel, headed straight for Grimgerde.

"Gah!" Leen switched to evasive maneuvers, dodging just in time for Lu's shot to make a massive crater in the ground where Grimgerde had been standing.

Debris and dirt ended up being kicked up into the air, blinding the surrounding area. Hilde used that to her advantage, charging head-on with Siegrune toward Leen. Leen's Frame Gear wasn't built for close-quarters combat, so getting too close would mean the end for her.

"You're mine!"

"Not so far, Hilde-dono!" Hilde's blade was blocked by a katana. Yae's Schwertleite revealed itself from the clouds of dirt.

Hilde's Frame Gear was very similar to Yae's, except Siegrune was more defense-oriented, while Schwertleite was more offense-oriented.

The purple samurai and the orange knight continued to trade blows, but both were at a stalemate.

Leen and her Grimgerde had gotten a good distance away and were now engaged in a long-range battle with Lu's Waltraute.

Leen's Gatling gun suddenly stopped spinning, it had overheated due to being used too long. Leen ejected the smoking weapon from her Frame Gear and carried on. Seemed she'd rather drop dead weight than carry a gun that she could use later.

Lu used the cooldown period to switch from her C-Unit to her B-Unit, charging in toward Leen with the heightened mobility granted to her.

Grimgerde opened up its shoulder missile pods, but by that point, Waltraute was already in too close. Grimgerde had been stabbed straight through the torso.

"Not bad... But I'm gonna take you with me!" Grimgerde extended its arms and held Waltraute tight, then opened up its damaged chest to reveal two surprise Gatling guns. Waltraute was practically hugged up against the weapons, which immediately began to spin up and fire a slew of bullets.

"Wh- No! No fair!" Waltraute was riddled with more holes than Swiss cheese. It fell to the ground and exploded into pieces, causing Grimgerde to detonate as well.

"Kokonoe Secret Style: Flying Swallow Rend!"

"Lestian Sacred Sword: Fifth Swirl!" Siegrune and Schwertleite continued to clash, ending it by striking each other through the chest at the same time.

"…It seems we have assured mutual destruction, we have…"

"What a shame." The two Frame Gears exploded into pieces, leaving nothing behind but wreckage. The battlefield was completely abandoned, all that remained was a smoldering waste.

"Simulation over. No survivors on either side. Draw. Opening hatch." The Frame Units all opened up at once.

As I looked around the Babylon facility and then back up at the monitor, the four girls hopped out of their VR pods.

"So yeah, that was a Frame Gear battle. Or rather, a simulation of one."

"Wow…"

"Really wow…" Elluka and Fenrir were still staring with their mouths agape.

"Good job!" I called out to the girls.

"It was another mutual kill, it was…"

"We keep doing that."

"I really thought I had you that time… Didn't expect you to take me out like that."

"You can't afford to be careless. The moment you're sure of your victory is the moment you need to be the most careful, Lu. You still have a few things to learn." I figured it was likely they'd end up drawing with the team matchups being what they were.

After looking at the battle footage, I realized we probably needed to improve Grimgerde's close-range abilities. If she couldn't deal with nearby enemies, that'd be bad. I decided to ask Rosetta about it later.

"So, what exactly do you think she can help with?" Doc Babylon stood by my side and motioned toward Elluka.

"Well, first of all, I'd like you to bring her up to speed on the magitech stuff this world has, but then I'd like to see if we can get some kind of communication device going."

"A communicator?"

"Yeah, but a special one. I want an object that can communicate between the regular world and the Reverse World. If you employ the same kind of Space-time magic used in the Dimensional Disruptor, it should be doable." I figured that'd be useful. That way we'd be able to know immediately if any mutants showed up in the Reverse World.

"So you mean to create an interdimensional smartphone?"

"Pretty much. Yeah. I think if we can set up some kind of relay station on either side, it'd help. There'd probably be a slight message delay, though." In that case, I'd probably need to give a smartphone to Nia from the Red Cats... Or maybe I'd be better off giving it to Est instead.

"When the two worlds become one, there won't be any need for a relay, you know." Even if that was true, we still needed one in the interim. As the scout motto goes, "Be prepared."

In other words, you always had to be ready to face any kind of threat in any kind of situation.

"I'll leave it to you, anyway. Let me know when it's finished."

"Sure. No problem. Oh, right... Whatever became of those magic trains in Felsen?"

"Uhh… I think they're almost done? The first two trains should be deployed in Belfast and Refreese respectively soon. We'll be informed when they're done." I was the one who had to transport the trains to the two countries, anyway.

The construction of a train line between Refreese and Belfast was well underway. They were using earth mages to flatten out the land.

If the Refreese-Belfast line worked out, then the next project would be a line between Lestia and Felsen. After that, we'd move to connect Belfast and Mismede.

It'd likely be used for hauling freight to begin with, rather than passengers. But who knew what the future would bring? I just hoped it'd work out.

I went down from Babylon and headed over to Olba's store. I was always fond of the Strand Company, since they dealt with things as small as capsule toys, to things as big as the Dverg mechs.

There were a few kids gathered in front of the store, playing with various little toys and trinkets.

"Ah, Your Highness! Greetings!"

"Hey, mister!" One older kid greeted me, which prompted the younger ones nearby to wave in unison.

"Hey there. I hope you're doing well!" I took out some snacks and candies from my [Storage], making some small talk with the kids before handing them over and heading indoors.

There was a benefit to staying in touch with kids. They often kept their ears to the grounds and knew subtle differences in the town. They heard the complaints of their parents and other rumors. Most of the stuff they said was completely useless, though.

When I entered the store, Olba greeted me and brought me to a back room.

"How's the progress on the Ether Vehicle going?"

"Ah, yes. I've given out several to various royal families. I'm just waiting for the various nobles to catch interest, now." Ether Vehicles were not cheap purchases. They were definitely not something you could just frivolously purchase, so Olba's idea was to plant them as some kind of status symbol.

"What about the model magic trains?"

"We're preparing a good number of them. We should have a great deal prepared by the time the real railways open." The benefit of selling toy versions and model versions of the trains was that we could use them to increase public awareness of the actual trains.

If other countries began their own railway projects, then demand for the Dvergs would also rise. Felsen had a lot of mages, though... It was unlikely they'd need many.

I spoke with Olba about a few more basic ideas like adding more toys to the capsules, different Ether Vehicle models, and so on. After that, I left.

It'd been a while since I just walked around town. It was certainly livelier than it was last time, and there were more buildings popping up here and there. That also meant there was a slight increase in crime, so we'd increased our patrols. Fortunately, nothing major had happened, so I wasn't too worried.

I headed away from the town center and walked toward the school. Fiana, the principal, came out to say hello.

Everything seemed to be going fine at the school. I asked her if they needed anything, and she said that they lacked instruments for their music classes, so I gave her a grand piano as a gift.

Apparently, they were just having Sakura come in to sing, or Sousuke come in to perform. I decided it'd be best if the teachers themselves could play the instruments on demand, too. Sousuke would be able to teach them the basics. If he couldn't, I'd certainly wonder why he had the divine position he had.

I also gave them some recorders and castanets for the students. They were pretty vital for elementary music class.

I spoke to Fiana for a bit about official matters, then headed outside. I found Mr. Mittens waiting for me at the door. I wondered what he wanted. "Meowlord! Halt fur a moment and hear my humble propawsition!"

"...I can't ban the Overlord from Brunhild, I'm sorry."

"Tsk... That's not what I want! I want companions!"

"Huh? Don't you have like... A whole army of cats?" Mr. Mittens had streetcats and housecats galore. There wasn't a feline in town that wasn't under his heel, and they were all working for the good of this town and its people.

Hell, there were more incidents where people annoyed the cats than the other way around.

"Those are my stalwart soldiers, sir! But I need equals! Understand?! I need Cat Siths, like me! Furry feline friends for fighting ferocious foes! I can't keep on managing this menagerie on my own!" Mr. Mittens ran up to me and clung to my leg. *You have your claws out, asshole!* "Isn't Sakura your master? You're... Meowing up the wrong tree, buddy."

"Sakura can't specifically call Cat Siths when she tries to summon familiars! I have three buddies that I need brought here! I'm begging you! I swear on at least three of my nine lives that I need this!"

"...Fine, whatever! I'll do it." For the first time in my life, I had witnessed a cat bowing. It was weird. To be honest, asking Mr. Mittens to manage every cat in town was unreasonable. Especially since he was meant to be helping Fiana every day, as well.

"I'll need to borrow your memories, then. Visualize those three friends of yours."

"Gotcha!" I grabbed Mr. Mitten's paws and pressed my thumbs up against his little pawpads. Then I pressed our foreheads together. If someone saw us now they'd probably wonder what the hell I was doing.

I saw the image of the three Cat Siths in my mind. I drew back and let go of his paws.

I set down the summoning circle in the school courtyard and poured my magic into it. A black mist began to form in the air until it condensed and finally dispersed.

Three small figures appeared in the middle of the circle where the black mist once was. Just as Mr. Mittens had done when he was summoned, the three felines pulled out their swords and raised them high into the air.

"All for one, and one for all!" One of them was an American shorthair. His face seemed stoic and serious. The other seemed like an elegant Siamese cat. The last one was a large, stocky Persian kitty.

They all wore the same stuff that Mr. Mittens did. They had feathered hats, big boots, capes, and rapiers. All three were clearly model cat knights.

"Good day to you, milord. Please grant us names." The American shorthair knelt down and spoke. He wasn't appending any stupid cat jokes to his dialogue, fortunately.

Thanks to Kohaku, I didn't need to fulfill any conditions to make a contract with summoned creatures like them, so all I had to do was give them names... I knew exactly what to call them.

"You're Athos. You can be Aramis, and you're Porthos."

"Very well!" Athos was the shorthair, Aramis was the Siamese, and Porthos was the Persian.

"Good meowning, people! It's been a while!"

"Oho, it's you! It's not actually morning, though... How've you been?"

"You seem the same as ever."

"Gahaha, you seem a little on the scrawny side, buddy. Sure you been eating right?" They were clearly old friends, so they were hitting it off well.

"Alright, well. You guys are gonna be helping Mr. Mittens, but otherwise, you're free to roam around town."

"...Mr. Mittens?"

"N-No! Erase that name from your minds right meow! I'm D'Artagnan!" Mr. Mittens flailed his arms around out of embarrassment. I had totally forgotten that Mr. Mittens wasn't his real name.

Since they were reuniting after a while, I gave them all a silver coin and told them to have fun on the town for a bit. All the bars in this area would be fine serving alcohol to the cats. Catnip-infused booze, of course.

Since Mr. Mittens had to finish up helping Fiana, I took the three cats to the bar ahead of him. I decided to teach them the ways around the streets, so I didn't use any fancy teleporting. It was already evening, so there were a few people out and about.

Nobody seemed to mind the sight of me and the three Cat Siths. Everyone was used to Mr. Mittens, after all. I only got a few confused glances from traveling merchants.

"This is quite a pleasant town."

"I'm glad it's to your liking." Athos cheerfully glanced around, but he seemed very alert. Aramis was already flirting with a nearby female cat. He was waving at her as she sat on a wall. Porthos, on the other hand, was hungrily staring at a stall that sold chicken skewers.

I think I had a good grasp of their personalities even though I hadn't known them long.

"So basically, you guys are gonna protect this town from the shadows just like Mr. Mittens does. Make sure you do your best, now."

"Very well!" We headed into the bar and found a bunch of men who had been drunk under the table by Suika. She was still sipping booze. The little gremlin was at it again… I had no idea how she was paying for booze when I'd canceled her allowance. She'd probably been winning bets against guys who thought they could outdrink her or something. "Ohh… Big bwoooo… How're… Hic… Youuuu?"

"I'm fine. How much have you had to drink?" She was completely wasted. I cleared up the glass bottles that were scattered around and shifted my eyes toward the barkeeper. He just looked away. *I see your game, mister. I'm sure she's bringing in a lot of income for you…*

"Let's get going, alright? Don't want Karina to catch you in this state."

"Bweeh… Hic! Fhiiine… But cawwy me…" She had free control over whether or not she got drunk, so it seemed to me like she just preferred being completely hammered. If she wanted to, she could make herself sober in a matter of minutes… But it seemed like half of the fun of drinking was in losing your inhibitions.

It was too late to blame her for it, so I just did what Suika said and put her on my shoulders. She really was a useless little gremlin.

"Hey barkeep, get some catnip sake for these guys. Mr. Mittens is coming over soon, too. So save some for him."

"Gotcha." The barkeep was a resident of Brunhild, so he didn't even blink twice at the sight of three cats ordering booze. He certainly got used to the swing of things quite fast.

I left the trio behind and headed back to the castle with Suika piggybacking on my shoulders. I felt like walking back on my own instead of using **[Gate],** for once.

The cool air blew along the path. It felt nice, in all honesty.

"Touya…"

"Yeah?"

"…I'm gonna barf…"

"[Gate]!" I charged toward the portal I'd opened up in front of me, but it was too late. *No way, this isn't happening!*

"…Bureegh@＊⁄＃Hrrrrk＄＋☆%Oooorkh…!!"

"OH HELL NOOOO!! AUUUUUGH! IT'S ALL DOWN MY NECK!" I made a silent oath at that moment. A promise to myself that I would never carry a drunk person ever again.

ıII Afterword

Hello again. How did you enjoy volume fourteen of In Another World With My Smartphone?

It's been quite a while since the anime aired now, hasn't it? A lot of time has passed without me even realizing it... Time flies like an arrow, after all.

I didn't watch the anime when was it was airing, but I picked it up on DVD and enjoyed it a lot. I even saw it got a lot of praise overseas, which was really nice to see. I am extremely grateful to all of you.

When I started thinking about writing this segment, I thought back to when Hobby Japan first approached me about making it a proper novel series. I still can't believe we managed thirteen volumes and then some more. It was only four years ago, you know? It's gone by unbelievably quickly for me.

The story's still going on, so I hope you join me for the rest of it.

At the time of writing this, it's August... And it's unbelievably hot. It's kind of getting in the way of my progress if I'm honest.

I have an air conditioner at home, but there isn't a unit in my bedroom... I only have an electric fan in there. That's why some nights I find it hard to fall asleep. I go to bed, and some mornings I wake up tired because of all the tossing and turning. I hope summer comes to an end soon. It's most unbearable.

I'm not good with heat, as I might've mentioned before. My body tends to get weaker around this time, too.

The only salvation here is that my job doesn't require me to go out much, so I'm at least spared from heatstroke.

But I think if this continues, I could end up falling ill. That's why I've decided that I might just sleep in my living room for a while. I expect things to get cooler around September, at least.

But man, a lot of stuff happened in this volume, huh? The Phrase Sovereign, Melle, finally awakened. From now on the Phrase won't just be enemies. Touya's meddling will lead to a lot of interesting situations for them. Ende's certainly gonna add to that, too.

The basic threat of the Phrase species is over at this point. The antagonists are now on a much broader scale, there's the threat of the wicked god and the mutants. I still don't think my story has that much of a heavy tone, though… So you should be able to read it just as lightly as ever.

I'd like to think my story is something worthy of being re-read now and then. If it isn't, then I'd like it to become that. So if you have my work on your bookshelf, please think of me every so often. I'll keep on doing my best for the sake of everyone who's been buying my stuff so far.

Oh right, the language that the king of Primula speaks is actually based on some wordplay I jumbled around. It's fine if you can't understand it, though. It's no big deal. It might get used again in the future, though.

Anyway, it's time to give my usual thanks.

To my illustrator, Eiji Usatsuka, thank you for sticking with me. There have been more and more characters coming up lately, so thanks for keeping track.

To the mech designer, Tomofumi Ogasawara, thanks so much for your incredible designs. I know there have been even more mechs coming up, so let me know if you need me to do anything. Thank you.

And of course, to K and the members of the Hobby Japan editorial staff, thank you so much for getting this book published.

And, of course, thank you to everyone who has followed my story on Shousetsuka ni Narou.

Patora Fuyuhara

In Another World With My Smartphone
Mecha Design Specs
Helmwige

Developer: Regina Babylon
Maintainer: High Rosetta
Administrator: Fredmonica
Height: 16.4m
Primary Color: Blue
Armaments: Multi-part Rifle, Vulcan Cannon x4, Triple-barrel Grenade Launcher x2, Blade Wing x2

Bone Frame Designer: Regina Babylon
Affiliation: Duchy of Brunhild
Compatible Pilot: Linze Silhoueska
Weight: 7.3t
Maximum Capacity: 2 People

A new special-model Frame Gear designed specifically for Linze. One of the Valkyrie Gears.
This Frame Gear can switch to a flight mode, giving it aerial superiority. It was primarily designed to intercept airborne foes.

Much like Grimgerde, it can sap its pilot's magic to load and fire artillery rounds. In an emergency situation, its wings can be detached and used as blades.

Developer: Regina Babylon

Maintainer: High Rosetta

Administrator: Fredmonica

Height: 17.5m

Primary Color: Black

Bone Frame Designer: Regina Babylon

Affiliation: Duchy of Brunhild

Compatible Pilot: Leen

Weight: 26.5t

Maximum Capacity: 1 Person

Armaments: Chest-compartment Gatling Gun x2, Six-pod Shoulder-mounted Missile Launcher x2, Seven-pod Knee-mounted Missile Launcher x2, Waist-mounted Machine Gun x2, Left-hand Vulcan Cannon Fingers, Right-arm Gatling Gun

A new special-model Frame Gear designed specifically for Linze. One of the Valkyrie Gears. A massive Frame Gear meant for large area-of-effect bombardment, Grimgerde can clear out multiple enemies at once with devastating magical and physical attacks. Its attack power far outclasses most other Frame Gears, but if it goes too long without stopping, it must shut down and enter a brief cooldown period.

Much like Ortlinde, it boasts a hefty defense, but its speed is comparatively pathetic.

In Another World With My Smartphone

Patora Fuyuhara
illustration・Eiji Usatsuka

15

**VOLUME 15
ON SALE
APRIL 2021!**

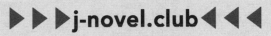

J-Novel Club Lineup

Ebook Releases Series List

A Lily Blooms in Another World
A Wild Last Boss Appeared!
Altina the Sword Princess
Amagi Brilliant Park
An Archdemon's Dilemma:
  How to Love Your Elf Bride
Arifureta Zero
Arifureta: From Commonplace
  to World's Strongest
Ascendance of a Bookworm
Beatless
Bibliophile Princess
Black Summoner
By the Grace of the Gods
Campfire Cooking in Another
  World with My Absurd Skill
Can Someone Please Explain
  What's Going On?!
Cooking with Wild Game
Crest of the Stars
Deathbound Duke's Daughter
Demon Lord, Retry!
Der Werwolf: The Annals of Veight
From Truant to Anime Screenwriter:
  My Path to "Anohana" and "The
  Anthem of the Heart"
Full Metal Panic!
Grimgar of Fantasy and Ash
Her Majesty's Swarm
Holmes of Kyoto
How a Realist Hero Rebuilt the
  Kingdom
How NOT to Summon a Demon
  Lord
I Refuse to Be Your Enemy!
I Saved Too Many Girls and Caused
  the Apocalypse
I Shall Survive Using Potions!
In Another World With My
  Smartphone
Infinite Dendrogram
Infinite Stratos
Invaders of the Rokujouma!?
Isekai Rebuilding Project
JK Haru is a Sex Worker in Another
  World
Kobold King
Kokoro Connect
Last and First Idol
Lazy Dungeon Master
Mapping: The Trash-Tier Skill That
  Got Me Into a Top-Tier Party

Middle-Aged Businessman, Arise in
  Another World!
Mixed Bathing in Another
  Dimension
Monster Tamer
My Big Sister Lives in a Fantasy
  World
My Instant Death Ability is So
  Overpowered, No One in This
  Other World Stands a Chance
  Against Me!
My Next Life as a Villainess: All
  Routes Lead to Doom!
Otherside Picnic
Outbreak Company
Outer Ragna
Record of Wortenia War
Seirei Gensouki: Spirit Chronicles
Sexiled: My Sexist Party Leader
  Kicked Me Out, So I Teamed Up
  With a Mythical Sorceress!
Slayers
Sorcerous Stabber Orphen:
  The Wayward Journey
Tearmoon Empire
Teogonia
The Bloodline
The Combat Butler and Automaton
  Waitress
The Economics of Prophecy
The Epic Tale of the Reincarnated
  Prince Herscherik
The Extraordinary, the Ordinary,
  and SOAP!
The Greatest Magicmaster's
  Retirement Plan
The Holy Knight's Dark Road
The Magic in this Other World is
  Too Far Behind!
The Master of Ragnarok & Blesser
  of Einherjar
The Sorcerer's Receptionist
The Tales of Marielle Clarac
The Underdog of the Eight Greater
  Tribes
The Unwanted Undead Adventurer
WATARU!!! The Hot-Blooded
  Fighting Teen & His Epic
  Adventures in a Fantasy World
  After Stopping a Truck with His
  Bare Hands!!

The White Cat's Revenge as
  Plotted from the Demon King's
  Lap
The World's Least Interesting
  Master Swordsman
Welcome to Japan, Ms. Elf!
When the Clock Strikes Z
Wild Times with a Fake Fake
  Princess

Manga Series:

A Very Fairy Apartment
An Archdemon's Dilemma:
  How to Love Your Elf Bride
Animeta!
Ascendance of a Bookworm
Bibliophile Princess
Black Summoner
Campfire Cooking in Another
  World with My Absurd Skill
Cooking with Wild Game
Demon Lord, Retry!
Discommunication
How a Realist Hero Rebuilt the
  Kingdom
I Love Yuri and I Got Bodyswapped
  with a Fujoshi!
I Shall Survive Using Potions!
Infinite Dendrogram
Mapping: The Trash-Tier Skill That
  Got Me Into a Top-Tier Party
Marginal Operation
Record of Wortenia War
Seirei Gensouki: Spirit Chronicles
Sorcerous Stabber Orphen:
  The Reckless Journey
Sorcerous Stabber Orphen:
  The Youthful Journey
Sweet Reincarnation
The Faraway Paladin
The Magic in this Other World is
  Too Far Behind!
The Master of Ragnarok & Blesser
  of Einherjar
The Tales of Marielle Clarac
The Unwanted Undead Adventurer

Keep an eye out at j-novel.club
for further new title
announcements!